JOHN
STEINBECK

COMPREHENSIVE RESEARCH
AND STUDY GUIDE

BLOOM'S
MAJOR
NOVELISTS

EDITED AND WITH AN
INTRODUCTION BY HAROLD BLOOM

CURRENTLY AVAILABLE

BLOOM'S MAJOR DRAMATISTS

Anton Chekhov

Henrik Ibsen

Arthur Miller

Eugene O'Neill

Shakespeare's Comedies

Shakespeare's Histories

Shakespeare's Romances

Shakespeare's Tragedies

George Bernard Shaw

Tennessee Williams

BLOOM'S MAJOR NOVELISTS

Jane Austen

The Brontës

Willa Cather

Charles Dickens

William Faulkner

F. Scott Fitzgerald

Nathaniel Hawthorne

Ernest Hemingway

Toni Morrison

John Steinbeck

Mark Twain

Alice Walker

BLOOM'S MAJOR SHORT STORY WRITERS

William Faulkner

F. Scott Fitzgerald

Ernest Hemingway

O. Henry

James Joyce

Herman Melville

Flannery O'Connor

Edgar Allan Poe

J. D. Salinger

John Steinbeck

Mark Twain

Eudora Welty

BLOOM'S MAJOR WORLD POETS

Geoffrey Chaucer

Emily Dickinson

John Donne

T. S. Eliot

Robert Frost

Langston Hughes

John Milton

Edgar Allan Poe

Shakespeare's Poems & Sonnets

Alfred, Lord Tennyson

Walt Whitman

William Wordsworth

BLOOM'S NOTES

The Adventures of Huckleberry Finn

Aeneid

The Age of Innocence

Animal Farm

The Autobiography of Malcolm X

The Awakening

Beloved

Beowulf

Billy Budd, Benito Cereno, & Bartleby the Scrivener

Brave New World

The Catcher in the Rye

Crime and Punishment

The Crucible

Death of a Salesman

A Farewell to Arms

Frankenstein

The Grapes of Wrath

Great Expectations

The Great Gatsby

Gulliver's Travels

Hamlet

Heart of Darkness & The Secret Sharer

Henry IV, Part One

I Know Why the Caged Bird Sings

Iliad

Inferno

Invisible Man

Jane Eyre

Julius Caesar

King Lear

Lord of the Flies

Macbeth

A Midsummer Night's Dream

Moby-Dick

Native Son

Nineteen Eighty-Four

Odyssey

Oedipus Plays

Of Mice and Men

The Old Man and the Sea

Othello

Paradise Lost

A Portrait of the Artist as a Young Man

The Portrait of a Lady

Pride and Prejudice

The Red Badge of Courage

Romeo and Juliet

The Scarlet Letter

Silas Marner

The Sound and the Fury

The Sun Also Rises

A Tale of Two Cities

Tess of the D'Urbervilles

Their Eyes Were Watching God

To Kill a Mockingbird

Uncle Tom's Cabin

Wuthering Heights

JOHN
STEINBECK

COMPREHENSIVE RESEARCH
AND STUDY GUIDE

BLOOM'S
MAJOR
NOVELISTS

**EDITED AND WITH AN INTRODUCTION
BY HAROLD BLOOM**

T23249

© 2000 by Chelsea House Publishers, a subsidiary of Haights Cross Communications.

Introduction © 2000 by Harold Bloom

Printed and bound in the United States of America.

3 5 7 9 8 6 4 2

Library of Congress Cataloging-in-Publication Data
John Steinbeck / edited and with an introduction by Harold Bloom.
    cm.—(Bloom's major novelists)
Includes bibliographical references and index.
ISBN 0-7910-5252-4 (hc)
Steinbeck, John, 1902-1968—Examination study guides.
I. Bloom, Harold.   II. Series.
PS3537.T3234Z71545   1999
813'.52—dc21   99-22479
                                                CIP

Chelsea House Publishers
1974 Sproul Road, Suite 400
Broomall, PA 19008-0914

The Chelsea House world wide web
address is www.chelseahouse.com

Contributing Editor: Aaron Tillman

11/22/02 $22.95

Contents

User's Guide

This volume is designed to present biographical, critical, and bibliographical information on the author's best-known or most important works. Following Harold Bloom's editor's note and introduction is a detailed biography of the author, discussing major life events and important literary accomplishments. A plot summary of each novel follows, tracing significant themes, patterns, and motifs in the work.

A selection of critical extracts, derived from previously published material from leading critics, analyzes aspects of each work. The extracts consist of statements from the author, if available, early reviews of the work, and later evaluations up to the present. A bibliography of the author's writings (including a complete list of all works written, cowritten, edited, and translated), a list of additional books and articles on the author and his or her work, and an index of themes and ideas in the author's writings conclude the volume.

~

Harold Bloom is Sterling Professor of the Humanities at Yale University and Henry W. and Albert A. Berg Professor of English at the New York University Graduate School. He is the author of over 20 books and the editor of more than 30 anthologies of literary criticism.

Professor Bloom's works include *Shelley's Mythmaking* (1959), *The Visionary Company* (1961), *Blake's Apocalypse* (1963), *Yeats* (1970), *A Map of Misreading* (1975), *Kabbalah and Criticism* (1975), and *Agon: Toward a Theory of Revisionism* (1982). *The Anxiety of Influence* (1973) sets forth Professor Bloom's provocative theory of the literary relationships between the great writers and their predecessors. His most recent books include *The American Religion* (1992), *The Western Canon* (1994), *Omens of Millennium: The Gnosis of Angels, Dreams, and Resurrection* (1996), and *Shakespeare: The Invention of the Human* (1998), a finalist for the 1998 National Book Award.

Professor Bloom earned his Ph.D. from Yale University in 1955 and has served on the Yale faculty since then. He is a 1985 MacArthur Foundation Award recipient, served as the Charles Eliot Norton Professor of Poetry at Harvard University in 1987–88, and has received honorary degrees from the universities of Rome and Bologna. In 1999, Professor Bloom received the prestigious American Academy of Arts and Letters Gold Medal for Criticism.

Currently, Harold Bloom is the editor of numerous Chelsea House volumes of literary criticism, including the series BLOOM'S NOTES, BLOOM'S MAJOR SHORT STORY WRITERS, BLOOM'S MAJOR POETS, MAJOR LITERARY CHARACTERS, MODERN CRITICAL VIEWS, MODERN CRITICAL INTERPRETATIONS, and WOMEN WRITERS OF ENGLISH AND THEIR WORKS.

Editor's Note

The Critical Extracts represent much of the best that has been thought and said about Steinbeck's major novels. On *The Grapes of Wrath* I find particularly useful the observations of Donald Pizer and Floyd C. Watkins, among others.

Jay Parini, Steinbeck's admirable biographer, joins Warren French among the most illuminative exegetes of *In Dubious Battle*.

Of *Mice and Men*, a difficult work for commentary, is admirably handled by Mark Spilka, as by the other critics reprinted here.

Introduction

HAROLD BLOOM

John Steinbeck remains a "popular novelist" in the most honorable sense of that phrase. *The Grapes of Wrath* is one of the classics of what might be called the American Religion, our indigenous national faith that is merely parodied by the Republican or Christian Right. Steinbeck's Okies are very much his own, and are not Protestants. Their Jesus Christ is the lapsed minister Jim Casy, whose disciple, Tom Joad, is a perpetual icon of American social revolution. Jim Casy's Bible consists of Ecclesiastes, as interpreted by way of Ralph Waldo Emerson and Walt Whitman. The Emersonian Oversoul inspires Jim Casy's prophecies, which sanctify sexuality and the Common life. Tom Joad, Steinbeck's most persuasive hero, is a populist prophet, Biblical rather than Marxist, and an authentic descendant of the politics of Thomas Jefferson and Andrew Jackson.

The Grapes of Wrath, whatever its aesthetic flaws, remains the authentic American novel of the now-vanishing Twentieth Century. The novel's heroines—Ma Joad and Rose of Sharon—are the truest prophets of the Ecclesiastes-vision. Ultimately skeptical, they endure because they have no expectations, and so they are beyond the consciousness of defeat. If there is an authentic representation in our literature of the perpetual American left, then it must be Ma Joad, with her iron faith that the common people, the insulted and injured, will prevail.

Neither *In Dubious Battle* nor *Of Mice and Men* has the permanence of *The Grapes of Wrath*, though both are likely to enjoy some half-life as social history. *In Dubious Battle*, though a Communist novel, is remarkably free of Marxist ideology, and remains a refreshingly American vision of social protest. It has, almost as strongly as *The Grapes of Wrath*, Steinbeck's rather original sense of men-in-groups, though it lacks the strong pathos of *Of Mice and Men*, which has a mythic intensity that redeems its failure as drama. All three share in Steinbeck's best quality, which is a passionate belief in the dignity of natural men and women, free insofar as they care for one another. ❁

Biography of John Steinbeck

John Ernst Steinbeck Jr. was born in Salinas, California, on February 27, 1902, to John Ernst Steinbeck and Olive Hamilton Steinbeck. John Jr. was the youngest of three siblings, with two older sisters, Esther and Elizabeth. His father was a farmer and the treasurer of Monterey County; his mother was a school teacher in the public school in Salinas, and throughout Steinbeck's childhood, she read to him from the world's most famous literature, cultivating in him a love of words and story. His favorite works were *Crime and Punishment, Paradise Lost,* and *Le Morte d'Arthur.* He also loved to read the King James Bible.

Besides books, Steinbeck also loved nature. Growing up in Salinas' fertile valley, he found much of the material that he would one day use in his books.

He graduated from Salinas high school in 1919, going on to Stanford University the following year. Prior to dropping out of Stanford, he published his first short stories in *The Stanford Spectator.*

Steinbeck moved to New York in 1925 and got a job as a reporter for the *American* newspaper. New York was not suited to his temperament, however, and the following year, he returned home to Salinas to devote his time to writing fiction. In 1929, *Cup of Gold* was published. The next year, he married Carol Henning and moved to Pacific Grove. In Pacific Grove he met Edward F. Ricketts, who became his confidant and critic. *Cup of Gold* failed to earn even the author's $250 advance, but Steinbeck was not discouraged.

In 1932 *The Pastures of Heaven* was published and in 1933, *To a God Unknown.* The same year *The Red Pony* appeared in two parts in *North American Review.* In 1935, *Tortilla Flat* was published, and as a result Steinbeck became more widely recognized. Soon after, he received $3,000 for the movie rights to this book. *In Dubious Battle* was published in 1936, and the following year *Of Mice and Men.*

While writing this last novel, Steinbeck ran into some unexpected trouble. While he and his wife were out one night, their Irish setter puppy destroyed nearly half of Steinbeck's manuscript. He had already labored long and hard, trying to create a new form of writing by combining a novel with a play's sparse language; thanks to his puppy, he needed another two months to re-create the destroyed passage.

Steinbeck used the money from his new-found success to travel throughout Europe. Upon his return, he traveled from Oklahoma to California with migrant workers, inspiring his Pulitzer prize–winning novel, *The Grapes of Wrath*. In 1940, he collected marine invertebrates in the Gulf of Mexico with Edward F. Ricketts. Based largely on this experience, in 1941 he published the book *Sea of Cortez*.

In 1942, Steinbeck divorced Carol Henning. The same year, he also published two books, *Bombs Away* and *The Moon Is Down*, both of which were set during World War II. He married Gwendolyn Conger in 1943 and moved to New York. During this time he was also working in Europe as a war correspondent for the *New York Herald Tribune*. The next year he wrote a script for Alfred Hitchcock's *Lifeboat*, and his son Thomas was born. The year after, the short novel *Cannery Row* was published, and in 1946, his son John was born.

Steinbeck traveled around Russia in 1947, and published *A Russian Journal* the following year. In 1947 he also published *The Wayward Bus* and *The Pearl*. Nineteen Forty Eight proved to be a difficult year for Steinbeck; he was divorced from his second wife Gwendolyn, and his close friend Edward F. Ricketts was killed in a car accident. In need of a change, Steinbeck started writing screenplays, including the largely political film *Viva Zapata!* In 1950, he married Elaine Scott.

Two years later, *East of Eden* was published, bringing Steinbeck back into the limelight. In 1954, *Sweet Thursday* was published, followed in 1957 by *The Short Reign of Pippin IV*. Steinbeck put out a collection of war dispatches in 1958 called *Once There Was a War*. In 1960, he went on a three-month tour of America with his dog Charley; this trip would become the basis of the book *Travels with Charley in Search of America* two years later. In 1961, Steinbeck's final novel, *The Winter of Our Discontent*, was published.

Steinbeck received the Nobel Prize for Literature in 1962 and the United States Medal of Freedom in 1964. In 1965, he traveled to Vietnam as a reporter for *Newsday*. In 1966, Steinbeck published his patriotic book *America and Americans*.

Two years later, on December 20, 1968, John Steinbeck died. He was buried in Salinas, California, the town of his birth. Since his death, various volumes of letters and journals have been published posthumously, though his literary identity will forever be linked with the keen social and political novels of the late 1930s. Although he never wrote an autobiography, each of his writings contain pieces of his life story. ❁

Plot Summary of
The Grapes of Wrath

The Grapes of Wrath, John Steinbeck's most famous work, tracks an Oklahoma farming family on a pilgrimage to the romanticized land of California. However, as Steinbeck moved through the Joads' story, he found that the narrative alone did not cover the entire picture he hoped to create. In order to include the material he felt was needed, he inserted chapters that summarize the Joads' general situation, rather than showing us their specific actions. These chapters describe such things as the background of the dust bowl, the highway that leads from Oklahoma to California, and the ownership of land in California. The story's main characters do not appear in these chapters, but the chapters are nevertheless important to the entire story, for not only do they extend the readers' understanding, they also contain symbols and foreshadowing that deepen the narrative.

The story opens in the hot, dry Oklahoma summer, as Tom Joad, who has been paroled from prison for manslaughter, hitches a ride in a rig to his family's farm. When Tom is dropped off, he walks through the dense clouds of unsettled dust and comes upon Jim Casy, his family's former preacher. Casy makes it clear that he is no longer a practicing preacher; he has decided that since everything and everybody is holy, he doesn't need to preach, since he can find holiness by being with people. Casy decides to join Tom on the walk to his family's farm.

When Casy and Tom arrive at the Joad homestead, they realize the house has been vacated and knocked from its foundation. As they attempt to determine what has taken place, they recognize Muley Graves, one of Tom's old neighbors, walking down the road. They reacquaint themselves with Muley, who wastes no time in explaining that the bank has forced everyone unable to pay their bills to leave their land. The corporations have control, and they are using tractors to till the soil. The Joad family has been staying at Tom's Uncle John's cabin until they move to California. Muley, on the other hand, has vowed to stay on his land and live by what ever means possible.

After spending the night outside the Joad's old place, Casy and Tom set off for Uncle John's cabin. Upon arriving at Uncle John's place, they encounter Pa (Tom's father), who is relieved Tom has made it out before the family leaves for California. Pa takes them in to surprise Ma, who is shocked, elated, and concerned all at once, afraid that Tom has escaped from prison. This question is raised by every member of the family, and each member is happy to hear that Tom has been let out on parole, with the exception of Al, one of Tom's younger brothers, who would prefer to hear an exciting jail break story. Grampa and Granma soon emerge from the barn, and Noah—another of Tom's brothers—along with his two youngest siblings, Ruthie and Winfield, all gather together for breakfast. At the table, the family tells Tom that Rose of Sharon, one of his sisters, is married to a man named Connie, and the two are expecting a child.

After breakfast, the family discusses their plans for departure. They have $200 and a truck, which they purchased for $75. The plan is to pack the entire family, including Connie, Tom, and Casy, and head to the fruitful land of California, where, they have been led to believe, labor is needed to pick oranges and grapes.

That night, the family makes a spontaneous decision to get on the road before dawn. Grampa, who decides that he no longer wants to go, has to be drugged with a bottle of "soothin' sirup," which Ma has for the youngest child, Winfield. They slip the medicine into Grampa's coffee and in no time he is fast asleep. The family packs up, piles into the "ancient overloaded Hudson," and sets off for California.

The Joad family travels from early morning throughout the day, settling down soon after dusk on the side of the road, where another family, the Wilsons, have pitched a tent for the evening. Here Grampa takes a turn for the worst, and ultimately dies inside the Wilsons's tent. Grampa's death acts as a bond between the two families, who decide to combine their resources and travel west together.

After traveling through the mountains of New Mexico, they wait out the next day before trying to cross the wide, hot Arizona desert. The Joads spend the afternoon at a camp, where people share tales of the ruthless life in California. They meet families who fled the cruel life there, spiteful families, stripped of their resources, their dreams, and their pride.

As dusk begins to settle, the Joads and the Wilsons get back on the road and continue their journey across the desert, stopping at a camp just inside the border of California. The Joad men seek refuge from the heat in a river flowing on the outskirts of the camp. After everyone has left the river, except Noah and Tom, Noah tells Tom that he's not going to travel any further; he's found his place and has made the decision to stay.

At this point the Wilson family and the Joad family say their final goodbyes. Sairy Wilson, Ivy Wilson's wife, has been growing weaker by the day and is unable to go any further. When the Joads get back on the road, Granma is also growing weak and mildly delirious, though Ma remains faithfully by her side. The family feels compelled to make it through the remainder of the desert before sunrise. Though discouraging tales of a dismal job market mix with the derogatory words of California locals, who make comments such as: "We don't want you goddamn Okies settlin' down," the Joads fight to remain hopeful.

When the family makes it past the desert and the sun starts to rise, revealing breathtaking scenery—fields of fruit as far as the eye can see—the family's moment of joy is quenched by the news that Granma did not make it through the night.

The Joads spend nearly all their money on the coroner's fee for Granma, before they make it to another settlement. A local contractor gets Tom, Casy, and some other members of the settlement riled up, and Casy kicks the contractor unconscious. Casy volunteers to take the entire blame and subsequently gets hauled off to jail. The local authorities claim they will burn the settlement down, which forces the Joads back on the road to look for another place to settle. Connie, Rose of Sharon's husband, decides to take off on his own.

After a couple of attempts to skirt the center of town, the Joads wind up in a government camp, where the laws are governed from the inside out, enforced through an internal committee of residents. The camp proves to be the nicest place they will ever stay, equipped with running water, flush toilets, a laundry area, and genuinely gracious people. The Joads remain at the camp for about a month, until it becomes painfully clear that there is not enough work for them to survive.

The Joads set out again, traveling north until their truck gets a flat. While changing the tire, another truck stops and tells them of a job picking peaches at a nearby ranch. Once the tire is fixed, they proceed directly to the ranch, along a road which is lined with police officers. The first day seems hopeful: the wages are high enough for them to earn enough money to eat, despite the elevated produce prices at the ranch-owned general store.

That evening, Tom sets off to investigate the police activity along the road, eventually coming across a group of men hiding in the woods. He soon discovers that Casy is among these men. Casy tells Tom that within a few days, hordes of new workers will arrive at the ranch and all the wages will be cut in half. While Casy is speaking, the group is approached by local officials. Casy makes an attempt to state his case, but before he can say too much, the officer drives a club into his skull and kills him. In an uninhibited reaction, Tom lunges at the officer, grabs his weapon, taking a few blows to his face before clubbing the man to death, and fleeing into the woods.

Tom makes it back to his family's camp that night. In the morning he discloses what has happened and makes arrangements to hide in the woods until his face has healed, hoping he can eventually work himself back into the labor force. The Joads continue to work on the ranch, picking peaches and making just enough money to feed their family. At night, Ma leaves a plate of food for Tom at a designated location. This continues until Ruthie gets into a fight with another girl; Ruthie tells the other girl that her brother, who has already killed two people, will make her pay. Tom's secret is out. Ma is forced to inform Tom and insist that he go off on his own, thus breaking up the family and breaking Ma's heart.

At this point the internal, social, and environmental forces with which the Joads have struggled begin to converge. The internal issues emerge quite literally inside Rose of Sharon's stomach, as she goes into a premature labor. While struggling to give birth, the hard California rains become unrelenting, flooding people inside their shelters and drowning the gears of the vehicles so that people can neither work nor move on.

After an exhausting, excruciating labor, Rose of Sharon's child is stillborn. Ma, unable to accept her family's complacent air of defeat, takes it upon herself to lead Rose of Sharon, Ruthie, and Winfield away from the drowning camp to seek shelter on higher ground.

The story comes to a close as Ma, Rose of Sharon, Ruthie, and Winfield find a barn on the top of a hill where they seek shelter. Once inside, they discover a young boy cowering in the corner of the barn next to a withered, older man. The boy's father is dying of starvation, having sacrificed all his food so the boy could eat. The boy explains that he had stolen some bread for his father, but the man threw it right back up. The boy goes on to ask, "You folks got money to git milk?" The story ends as Rose of Sharon, encouraged by Ma, offers her breast to the starving man. ❀

List of Characters in
The Grapes of Wrath

Tom Joad is the first primary character the reader encounters. He has served time in jail for manslaughter and is out on parole. He quickly proves to be the backbone of the Joad family, acting both as chief engineer for the family automobile and as their guiding voice throughout their pilgrimage to California. Tom is forced to leave the family after his murderous reaction to the unjust killing of Jim Casy.

Ma Joad acts as the crutch for the family, seeing to the family's most basic needs, while also providing a rational source of motivation and strength that keeps the family together until the very end.

Pa Joad (**Tom Joad Sr.**) does his best to aid the family's pilgrimage, though his inability to adapt to the perpetually changing surroundings forces him to take a back seat to his sons and his wife.

Al Joad is a feisty, hormone-driven teen, who has a great deal of admiration for his older brother Tom, particularly after Tom kills a man. Al's knowledge of cars proves valuable throughout the pilgrimage to California.

Uncle John Joad provides shelter for the family before their journey west. He is consumed by his sinful nature, allowing the burden of his guilt to dictate his actions.

Rose of Sharon Joad is pregnant and recently married to Connie Rivers when the pilgrimage begins. Her baby is born stillborn and the novel concludes with her breast-feeding a starving man.

Ruthie and **Winfield Joad** are the youngest of Tom's siblings. Ruthie's words, suggesting to another girl that her brother will kill her just as he has done already, force Tom to finally flee from the family.

Granma and **Grampa Joad** both die on the way to California. They are symbols of the end of the Joad's Oklahoma farm life.

Noah Joad is Tom's awkward younger brother. Noah decides to leave the family after crossing the border into California.

Jim Casy is the Joads' former minister who is perpetually consumed by the inconsistencies of religion, as well as the power of the human spirit. He takes a final stand against the injustices of the California labor force before he is killed.

Connie Rivers is Rose of Sharon's husband who travels to California with the Joad family After grappling with feelings of complacency and inadequacy, he leaves his wife and the Joad family.

Muley Graves is the first one to tell Tom and Jim Casy what has taken place with all the small local farms. He remains behind in Oklahoma, unwilling to be driven out of his home state.

Ivy and **Sairy Wilson** are the husband and wife who travel with the Joads toward California. Sairy's lack of strength prevents them from finishing the journey with the Joads. ❀

Critical Views on
The Grapes of Wrath

FREDERIC I. CARPENTER ON THE GROUP VS.
THE INDIVIDUAL

[Frederic I. Carpenter has taught at the University of
Chicago, Harvard University, and the University of Cali-
fornia, Berkeley. His works include: *Emerson Handbook,
Emerson and Asia, American Literature and the Dream,* and
The American Myth. In this excerpt, Carpenter discusses the
philosophical and poetic elements in *The Grapes of Wrath.*]

Upon the foundation of this old American idealism Steinbeck has
built. But the Emersonian oversoul had seemed very vague and very
ineffective—only the individual had been real, and he had been concerned more with his private soul than with other people. *The
Grapes of Wrath* develops the old idea in new ways. It traces the
transformation of the Protestant individual into the member of a
social group—the old "I" becomes "we." And it traces the transformation of the passive individual into the active participant—the idealist becomes pragmatist. The first development continues the poetic
thought of Walt Whitman; the second continues the philosophy of
William James and John Dewey.

"One's-self I sing, a simple separate person," Whitman had proclaimed. "Yet utter the word Democratic, the word En-Masse." Other
American writers had emphasized the individual above the group.
Even Whitman celebrated his "comrades and lovers" in an essentially
personal relationship. But Steinbeck now emphasizes the group
above the individual and from an impersonal point of view. Where
formerly American and Protestant thought has been separatist,
Steinbeck now faces the problem of social integration. In his novel
the "mutually repellent particles" of individualism begin to cohere.

"This is the beginning," he writes, "from 'I' to 'we.'" This is the
beginning, that is, of reconstruction. When the old society has been
split and the Protestant individuals wander aimlessly about, some
new nucleus must be found, or chaos and nihilism will follow. "In
the night one family camps in a ditch and another family pulls in
and the tents come out. The two men squat on their hams and the

women and children listen. Here is the node." Here is the new nucleus. "And from this first 'we,' there grows a still more dangerous thing: 'I have a little food' plus 'I have none.' If from this problem the sum is 'We have a little food,' the thing is on its way, the movement has direction." A new social group is forming, based on the word "en masse." But here is no socialism imposed from above; here is a natural grouping of simple separate persons.

By virtue of his wholehearted participation in this new group the individual may become greater than himself. Some men, of course, will remain mere individuals, but in every group there must be leaders, or "representative men." A poet gives expression to the group idea, or a preacher organizes it. After Jim Casy's death, Tom is chosen to lead. Ma explains: "They's some folks that's just theirself, an' nothin' more. There's Al [for instance] he's jus' a young fella after a girl. You wasn't never like that, Tom." Because he has been an individualist, but through the influence of Casy and of his group idea has become more than himself, Tom becomes "a leader of the people." But his strength derives from his increased sense of participation in the group.

From Jim Casy, and eventually from the thought of Americans like Whitman, Tom Joad has inherited this idea. At the end of the book he sums it up, recalling how Casy "went out in the wilderness to find his own soul, and he found he didn't have no soul that was his'n. Says he foun' he jus' got a little piece of a great big soul. Says a wilderness ain't no good 'cause his little piece of a soul wasn't no good 'less it was with the rest, an' was whole." Unlike Emerson, who had said goodbye to the proud world, these latter-day Americans must live in the midst of it. "I know now," concludes Tom, "a fella ain't no good alone."

To repeat: this group idea is American, not Russian; and stems from Walt Whitman, not Karl Marx. But it does include some elements that have usually seemed sinful to orthodox Anglo-Saxons. "Of physiology from top to toe I sing," Whitman had declared, and added a good many details that his friend Emerson thought unnecessary. Now the Joads frankly discuss anatomical details and joke about them. Like more common people, they do not abscond or conceal. Sometimes they seem to go beyond the bounds of literary decency: the unbuttoned antics of Grandpa Joad touch a new low in folk-comedy. The movies (which reproduced most of the realism of the book) could not quite stomach this. But for the most part they preserved the spirit of the book, because it was whole and healthy.

—Frederic I. Carpenter, "The Philosophical Joads," *College English* 2, no. 4 (January 1941): pp. 318–320.

STUART L. BURNS ON THE NOVEL'S ENDING

[Stuart L. Burns is a professor of 20th-century American Literature at Drake University in Des Moines, Iowa. In addition to scholarly essays, his works include *Whores Before Descartes: Assorted Prose and Poetry*. In this excerpt, Burns uses the turtle as a metaphor for the Joad family.]

There are certain similarities between the turtle and the Joads, of course: it is heading southwest, as will they; the highway (but not the same highway) is a formidable obstacle to both; and the overloaded Hudson certainly travels at a turtle's pace. But consider the very real and thematically more meaningful distinctions. The turtle has an instinctive sense of purpose and direction; it turns "aside for nothing." And while one cannot know for certain where the turtle is going or what it intends to do when it gets there, the context clearly implies that it *will* get there and accomplish whatever it has instinctively set out to do. The Joads, on the other hand, head southwest due to circumstances beyond their control. They have at first no desire to move at all, and throughout a nostalgia for the Oklahoma farm they were forced to leave. And only an unflagging optimist would connect their concluding situation, or for that matter their future prospects, with any concrete achievement. But perhaps the most significant distinction between the turtle and the Joads is that, whereas the former plays a fertilizing role to the "sleeping life waiting to be dispersed," the life that Rosasharn carries is delivered premature and stillborn. Twelve Joads spanning three generations (thirteen spanning four if one counts the unborn baby) begin the journey; although ten presumably survive, only six are together at the end. The emphasis is on attrition, not continuance.

If one examines subsequent passages in the novel where the turtle is alluded to, the difference between the positive thrust of the parable and the negative thrust of the narrative becomes even clearer. Two characters, Tom Joad and Jim Casy, are specifically associated with the turtle. Tom picks it up and carries it with him for a while (to the northeast, opposite the turtle's intended direction); and Casy's physical description is suggestive of a turtle. He has a "long head, bony, tight of skin, and set on a neck as stringy and muscular as a celery stalk." His "heavy . . . protruding" eyeballs with lids stretched to cover them are decidedly reptilian. That Tom and Casy should be closely associated with the turtle is appropriate inasmuch as, of the thirteen people who trek west in the Hudson, these two do develop a sense of purpose and direction akin to the turtle's. But the analogy has its limits. The turtle survives its encounter with the hostile forces of civilization. Indeed, the truck which swerves to hit it actually flips it across the highway, aiding it in this hazardous crossing. Casy, who has no protective shell into which he can withdraw his head, has it crushed by a pick handle wielded by the leader of the mob at the Hooper ranch. And while Tom survives on this occasion, his future—a hunted ex-convict turned labor agitator—bodes nothing but ill. The text suggests that the turtle will survive because it expends its energies totally in its self-interest; Casy dies because he devotes his energies to helping others.

This distinction between self-interest and humanitarianism is further illustrated in another brief scene in which Granma is associated with the turtle. The red ant which crawls "over the folds of loose skin on her neck" while she is dying recalls the ant the turtle crushes inside its shell. But, whereas the turtle reacts savagely and effectively, Granma is able to do no more than feebly scratch her face. To be sure, Ma Joad crushes the ant "between thumb and forefinger," in a gesture reminiscent of the turtle's action. But this only reinforces the point that, as Tom Joad states later, "a fella ain't no good alone."

—Stuart L. Burns, "The Turtle or the Gopher: Another Look at the Ending of *The Grapes of Wrath*," *Western American Literature* 9, no. 1 (Spring 1974): pp. 54–55.

[Horst Groene is a professor of English at Kiel University. In addition to his work on Steinbeck, he has published widely on American writers such as Sherwood Anderson, J. D. Salinger, and Tennessee Williams. In this excerpt, Groene talks about Steinbeck's portrayal of the American farmer.]

The impact of the ideal figure of the Western yeoman farmer is also discernible in the characterization of the Joads and other tenant farmers, who, regardless of their coarse and unrefined speech and manners, appear basically good and virtuous. They are portrayed as generous and helpful people, adhering to their moral code, displaying considerable strength of character in the face of constant adversity and preserving their dignity in spite of growing hostility. Through his sympathetic treatment of the Joads and other dispossessed farmers, Steinbeck has created a more appealing picture of the Western farmer and his plight than did his nineteenth century forerunners Joseph Kirkland, E. W. Howe and Hamlin Garland.

Steinbeck's agrarian ideals apparently made him also resent the mechanization and industrialization of agriculture with its concomitant absentee ownership. In *The Grapes of Wrath* machines destroy the close bond between Man and Nature, make the tenant farmer redundant and force him off the land so that he becomes a shiftless migrant worker. It is above all the tractor which threatens the self-sufficient and satisfying way of life of the small farmer and which becomes something approaching a new symbol of the traditional "anti-pastoral counterforce of industrialism," which Leo Marx has described with such wealth of detail in his investigation of the impact of modern technology on American thinking.

Nevertheless, nineteenth century ideals could not provide adequate solutions to the problems posed by the agricultural revolution. Steinbeck, too, had to acknowledge this at the end of his novel—in spite of his agrarian predilections. For in California the Joads are soon confronted with the situation that half a century before prompted Frederick Jackson Turner to write his great essay "The Significance of the Frontier in American History" (1893): the frontier is closed, the dream of owning a small piece of land must be buried as wishful thinking. Even worse, living conditions deteriorate all the time and the family slowly dissolves in spite of Ma Joad's efforts.

Tom their leader, who feels such strong attachment to the soil, is forced to flee, and the novel ends with the remnants of the Joad Clan trying to survive the flood-like rains in the box car and barn. True, critics are agreed that *The Grapes of Wrath* ends on a somewhat optimistic note: Rose of Sharon's gesture of help can be understood as a sign of the indestructible life force of the people. But it is undeniable that such an interpretation has to rely heavily on the symbolic aspects of this conclusion, whereas on the level of concrete action the Joads' situation is quite hopeless.

—Horst Groene, "Agrarianism and Technology in Steinbeck's *The Grapes of Wrath*," *Southern Review* 9, no. 1 (March 1976): pp. 27–28.

James D. Brasch on Old Testament Skepticism

[James D. Brasch is a professor of English at McMaster University in Ontario. In addition to his work on Steinbeck, Brasch has also written on the works of Ernest Hemingway. In this excerpt, Brasch addresses the notion of faith within the Joad family.]

Just as the Old Testament Preacher realized that the common labourers' real remuneration lay in the satisfactions which they received from honest toil, so Steinbeck's characters consoled themselves with thoughts of their ultimate survival and at least partial triumph. Just as Koheleth recognized that "There is no end of all the people" (4:16), Ma cautions Tom in one of the focal passages of the novel:

> "Easy," she said. "You got to have patience. Why, Tom—us people will go on livin' when all them people is gone. Why, Tom we're the people that live. They ain't gonna wipe us out. Why, we're the people—we go on."

When Tom asks her how she knows this, her faith triumphs over his skepticism as she answers, "I don't know how," and this intuitive assertion leaves the Joads in a mystical relation to their surroundings from which they gain strength even in moments of intense despair. Considered in the light of Ecclesiastes, the passage reflects a proletarian recognition of the importance of labour to the kingdom of Israel and not some vague echo of Ralph Waldo Emerson or Carl Sandburg. The biblical tone is emphasized in several intercalations as faith in proletarian progress, and triumph is prophesized in biblical syntax:

> This you may say of man—when theories change and crash, when schools, philosophies, when narrow dark alleys of thought, national religions, economics, grow and disintegrate, man reaches, stumbles forward, painfully, mistakenly sometimes. Having stepped forward, he may slip back, but only half a step, never the full step back. *This you may say and know it and know it.* [My italics.]

The passage continues in a biblical tone and rhythm revealing Steinbeck's insistence on the biblical precedent, as he warns of oppression. There is strength for the poor in this knowledge.

Steinbeck's attitude toward justice was significantly established, moreover, by the Old Testament skeptic who pleaded for justice in the tradition of the great prophets of Israel. Virtually alone, he recognized the futility of expecting justice on this earth. Koheleth had attempted to console his poor with the knowledge that their labour rendered them the basic fabric of the nation, but he was quite aware that "oppression maketh a wise man mad" (7:7). It was this inevitable result of excessive persecution and eternal frustration that Steinbeck also wanted to avoid in California. The ominous predictions in *The Grapes of Wrath* are legion. The titular passage of the novel warns of impending disaster in biblical diction and tone and with imagery from Ecclesiastes:

> In the eyes of the people there is the failure; and in the eyes of the hungry there is a growing wrath. In the soul of the people the grapes of wrath are filling and growing heavy, growing heavy for the vintage.

—James D. Brasch, "*The Grapes of Wrath* and Old Testament Skepticism," *San Jose Studies* 3, no. 2 (May 1977): pp. 20–21.

[Floyd C. Watkins is a Professor of English at Emory University. He is the author of *The Flesh and the Word, The Death of Art,* and various selections on Robert Penn Warren and Thomas Wolfe. In this excerpt, Watkins exposes the errors and inconsistencies contained in *The Grapes of Wrath.*]

Besides the factual errors, there are a number of improbable occurrences in *The Grapes of Wrath.* An ant runs "into the soft skin inside the shell" of the "land turtle," and the terrapin crushes it. It would be close in there, but not insecticidal. The Joads' house is pushed down by a tractor. I learned of one such occurrence near Caddo, Oklahoma, in the 1940s, but again the event was not sufficiently representative for Steinbeck to use it in fiction aiming at social truth.

The variety of geography and the diversity of cultures in the United States make a single national literature impossible. In a sense there is no national literary history in America, but there are many different ones. Certain things are nationwide; I believe doves appear all over the country. When a novelist uses only objects that are as universal as the dove, he does not describe a region. Steinbeck did not know Oklahoma well enough to attempt to write a novel about it. The particulars he uses are either from California, or universal, or wrong. The Joads are a kind of people that Steinbeck did not know very well; they have individual identities, but they are not peculiarly Oklahoman. Such things as scissortails and horned toads are not found in *The Grapes of Wrath.* Nor are Indians, and it is impossible to travel far in Oklahoma without seeing some of them. The novel here is incomplete if not erroneous. On one occasion Steinbeck publishes his ignorance of his subject. Casy and Tom Joad see a "dry watering trough, and the proper weeds that should grow under a trough were gone." Now Faulkner would know what kind of weeds were there. The botanical life of Yoknapatawpha County is lush with honeysuckle, heaven trees, dog fennel, jimson weeds, wistaria, verbena, and many other particular plants. "Proper weeds" is plain bad writing. In this case Steinbeck did not even provide a dove, much less a scissortail.

The Grapes of Wrath is sometimes wrong and often vague, but many details also ring true. Much of the nature is right. Water did have "surface dust" after a storm. Jackrabbits do have boils. A hungry man could eat skunk meat after washing the musk off the fur. The anatomy of the hog-killing is right. The gophers and wild oats and the big owl with a "white underside" are native of Oklahoma. Some unusual customs in the novel were practiced by the poor people during the depression. Farmers lashed barbed wire to fence posts with baling wire because they had no money to buy nails or staples. Urine is used as a medicine by Oklahomans. Farmers have urinated on animals to stop bleeding, rubbed urine as a cure on horses' sores, and used urine as a medicine for earache. That "picture of an Indian girl in color, labeled Red Wing," is on a can of Calumet Baking Powder, an item once found in every farm kitchen.

So what if the facts are wrong and omitted? Does that make the fiction bad? In a way it does because it becomes allegorical, invented. It is fantasy, and it is false. The people are usually wrong in much the same way the facts are. They live in a flat universality instead of among the clutter of their daily lives. Poverty is not an absence of things in the daily world. The poor have different kinds of things from those who are more fortunate, but they may be surrounded with objects which depict them, as in homes in a junkyard. But Steinbeck's Okies are too much without objects.

> —Floyd C. Watkins, "Flat Wine from *The Grapes of Wrath.*" In *In Time and Place: Some Origins of American Fiction* (Athens, GA: University of Georgia Press, 1977): pp. 22–24.

DONALD PIZER ON THE ENDURING POWER OF THE JOADS

[Donald Pizer has been the Pierce Butler Professor of English at Tulane University. He has written extensively on American Literary Naturalism. In this excerpt, Pizer discusses the strength and resiliency of the Joad family.]

The care with which Steinbeck molds our sense of the primitive strength of the Joads early in the novel is especially revealed in two areas of their experience. The Joads are attuned to solving the problems of their lives without outside aid. They raise and prepare their own food, they make their own clothes, and they create and maintain their own special form of transportation. We thus come to accept that the Joads are latter-day pioneers, that the myth of the self-sustaining pioneer family still lives in them. But the Joads not only solve problems by the exercise of individual skills but also by the maintenance of a group strength and efficiency. Here Steinbeck is at pains to dramatize his phalanx notion of the distinctive identity of the group. So, for example, in the family councils just before departure or soon after Grandpa's death, the family when it meets to solve its problems becomes a powerful and cohesive single body, "an organization of the unconscious. They obeyed impulses which registered only faintly in their thinking minds."

The Joads are folk as well as primitives; that is, we also experience the comic and the ritualized in their naturalness. For example, the three generations of the Joads constitute a gallery of family folk types: earthy and querulous grandparents, eccentric and even occasionally demented uncles and brothers, cocky and sexually vibrant late adolescents, and overcurious and problem-creating children. Above all, the Joads contain the archetypal center of the folk family, the mother as source of love, wisdom, and strength. The Joads as folk salt the novel with the sexuality and excrementality of folk humor and with the ritualized forms of folk life, particularly of courtship and death. Some of the folk attributes and experiences of the Joads have both a Dickensian predictability of repetitive motif and a freakish humor characteristic of Erskine Caldwell's portrayal of poor whites. (The Joads' discovery of the flush toilet is pure Caldwell.) But the folk element in the lives of the Joads, when combined with the central strain of their primitivism, contributes to rather than diminishes our sense of their basic humanity. The earthiness and humor of the Joads as folk permit Steinbeck to avoid the heavy breathing and lush primitivism of his early fiction—notably of *To a God Unknown*—and encourage us to respond to them not only as symbols but as "real" people.

The Joads as primitive folk appear to be opposed by the life-denying forces of the mechanical, institutional, and intellectual. In Oklahoma these forces are allegorized by the banks and corporations which have the law and wealth on their side but which lack the human attributes of understanding and compassion. The forces are symbolized above all by the impersonal mechanical tractor which destroys the farmers' homes and by the anonymous car which attempts to run over the turtle as it goes about its "business" of spreading the seed of life. Yet the mechanical and the commercial are not inherently evil. The Joads' jerry-built truck soon becomes a symbol of family unity as well as a means of fulfilling their striving for a better life. And the small businessmen along the road and the small California ranchers are themselves threatened with destruction. If the tractor were owned and used by the Joads, Steinbeck tells us, it would be a beneficial mechanical force. The real evils in the Joads' life are thus not the abstractions of the mechanical or the institutional but the human failings of fear, anger, and selfishness. Those who cheat or beleaguer or harass the Joads in Oklahoma and on the road and in California may symbolize the opposition of the structured in life to the natural but they are above all greedy or frightened men who wish to preserve or add to what they own. Steinbeck's depiction of this essentially human conflict suggests that his attempt in *The Grapes of Wrath* was not to dramatize a labored and conventional primitivistic ethic. It was rather to engage us, within the context of primitivistic values, in one of the permanent centers of human experience, that of the difficulty of transcending our own selves and thereby recognizing the nature and needs of others.

—Donald Pizer, "John Steinbeck: *The Grapes of Wrath.*" In *Twentieth-Century American Literary Naturalism: An Interpretation* (Carbondale and Edwardsville: Southern Illinois University Press, 1982): pp. 69–70.

LOUIS OWENS ON THE SEARCH FOR EDEN

[Louis Owens is a Professor of Literature at the University of California at Santa Cruz. His works include: *John Steinbeck's Re-Vision of America* and *"The Grapes of Wrath": Trouble in the Promised Land.* In this excerpt, Owens discusses the techniques that Steinbeck employs to avoid sentimental attachment to his characters.]

While the trials of the Joads engage us, even excite our admiration and pity, Steinbeck takes pains to deny us the luxury of sentimental attachment. The Joads, including even the ultimately heroic and Christ-like Casy, are no better, no greater, no less human than they should be. Nor are any of the other migrants in the novel.

More important than either Steinbeck's illumination of the human failings of his characters on such limited levels or his use of the interchapters as distancing devices is his care to emphasize the migrants' culpability, their portion of responsibility for what has happened to the land and to themselves. Certainly Steinbeck makes it clear that the sharecroppers are victimized by an inhuman economic monster that tears at the roots of Jeffersonian agrarianism. However, when Steinbeck causes his representative migrant voice to plead with the owners for a chance to remain on the land, he qualifies the celebrated Jeffersonian agrarianism and love-for-the-land by tainting the croppers' wish: "Get enough wars and cotton'll hit the ceiling," the cropper argues. A willingness to accept war and death as the price for further cottoning out of the land is difficult to admire on any level. And Steinbeck goes a step further, to make it clear that the migrants are firmly fixed in a larger, even more damning American pattern. Though the tenants have tried to persuade the owners to let them hang on, hoping for a war to drive up cotton prices, the tenant-voice also warns the owners: "But you'll kill the land with cotton." And the owners reply: "We know. We've got to take cotton quick before the land dies. Then we'll sell the land. Lots of families in the East would like to own a piece of land." With their words the westering pattern of American history is laid bare: we arrive on the Atlantic seaboard seeking Eden only to discover a rocky and dangerous paradise with natives who aggressively resent the "discovery" of their land; the true Eden must therefore lie ever to the west, over the next hill, across the next plain, until finally we reach the Pacific Ocean and, along with Jody's grandfather in *The Red Pony,* we end up shaking our fists at the Pacific because it stopped us, breaking the pattern of displacement, a pattern put into focus in Walt Whitman's poignant query in "Facing West from California's Shores": "But where is what I started for so long ago? / And why is it yet unfound?"

That the croppers are part of this pattern becomes even more evident when the representative tenant voice informs us that their fathers had to "kill the Indians and drive them away." And when the tenants add, "Grampa killed Indians, Pa killed snakes for the land," we should hear a powerful echo of the Puritan forebears who wrested the wilderness from the Satanic serpent and his Indian servants, killing and displacing the original inhabitants of the new Canaan.

It is difficult to feel excessive sorrow for these ignorant men who are quite willing to barter death to maintain their place in the destructive pattern of American expansion, a pattern that has ravaged a continent. That Steinbeck thought long about the American phenomenon of destroying the Garden just discovered in the search for an even better Garden is suggested in his declaration more than a decade later that in *East of Eden*, his great investigation of the myth of America, "people dominate the land, gradually. They strip it and rob it. Then they are forced to try to replace what they have taken out."

—Louis Owens, "The Culpable Joads: Desentimentalizing *The Grapes of Wrath*." In *Critical Essays on Steinbeck's The Grapes of Wrath*, ed. John Ditsky (Boston: G. K. Hall, 1989): pp. 111–112.

STEPHEN RAILTON ON THE JOADS AND THEIR OPPRESSORS

[Stephen Railton is a professor of English at the University of Virginia. He is the author of *Fenimore Cooper: A Study of His Life and Imagination*, as well as a comprehensive study on the major prose works of the American Renaissance as performances. In this excerpt, Railton addresses how the lack of sentimentality gives the book an honest feel.]

Perhaps the truest thing about the novel is its refusal to sentimentalize the life in the Midwest from which the Joads and the other families they meet have been dispossessed. When their dream of a golden future out West is destroyed by the brutal realities of migrant life in California, the past they left at the other end of Route 66 appeals to them as the paradise they have been driven from. When the novel winds up at the Hooper Ranch, the place seems as infernal as Simon Legree's plantation in *Uncle Tom's Cabin*. The armed guards, the filthy conditions, the edge of outright starvation on which Hooper Ranches, Inc., is content to keep the pickers—Steinbeck does want to expose this as one of the darkest places of the earth. At no point in the novel do the Joads feel further from "home," but Steinbeck also wants us to see how much Hooper's farm in California has in common with the Joad farm in Oklahoma that Tom had been trying to get back to at the beginning.

There is, for instance, a wire fence around both farms. The Joads didn't really need a fence, Tom tells Casy, but "Pa kinda liked her there. Said it give him a feelin' that forty was forty." And Pa got the wire by taking advantage of his own brother. That is Steinbeck's point; that is what both fences delimit. We hear just enough about the Joads' earlier life in Oklahoma to recognize that they lived on their forty acres with essentially the same narrowly selfish values as Hooper on his much larger orchard. The Sooners took their land by force from the Indians, just as the large owners in California took theirs from the Mexicans. In both places, what prevailed was the "right" of the strongest—or say, the greediest. The Joads even stole the house they are evicted from. Grampa hangs onto the pillow he stole from Albert Rance with the same fierceness that the owners display in defense of their ill-gotten profits. Steinbeck's antagonist in the novel is not the group of large owners, but rather the idea of ownership itself. It is at the Hooper Ranch that Ma, on the verge of despair, grows most sentimental about the past:

> They was the time when we was on the lan'. They was a boundary to us then. Ol' folks died off, an' little fellas come, an' we was always one thing—we was the fambly— kinda whole and clear.

Given what the Joads have been through since leaving home, it is impossible not to sympathize with her nostalgia. But finally, for Steinbeck, any kind of boundary—whether it's drawn around forty acres or forty thousand, around a family or a class—is wrong. And it is "the quality of owning" that builds boundaries, that "freezes you forever into 'I,' and cuts you off forever from the 'we.'"

—Stephen Railton, "Pilgrims' Politics: Steinbeck's Art of Conversion." In *New Essays on The Grapes of Wrath*, ed. David Wyatt (Cambridge: Cambridge University Press, 1990): pp. 30–32.

Plot Summary of
In Dubious Battle

In Dubious Battle contains both a specific and a general narrative. On the one hand are the events of the individual characters' lives as they become involved with an apple pickers' strike in the early 1930s; the reader cares about the outcome for the story's characters. On the other hand, however, Steinbeck is telling a more generic story about the conflict between idealist aims and violent means.

The story opens inside Jim Nolan's urban apartment, moments before he heads out to the local Communist Party office and commits himself to active duty. In the office, Jim meets Harry Nilson, who explains the initiation procedure and asks a series of questions concerning his reasons for wanting to join the party. Jim answers that his father, who was killed fighting for occupational justice, is the driving reason. He also explains that he is starving for something to believe in; "I feel dead," he says.

After spending the night in the party office, Harry Nilson brings Jim to the main party location, where he meets a number of field workers, including Mac, who becomes his closest confidant, traveling partner, and mentor. Jim is also introduced to Joy, an eccentric, borderline insane radical who has been beaten on numerous occasions; the most severe beating was a series of blows to his head with brass knuckles. Jim also meets Dick, a charismatic field veteran who is equally as dedicated as Joy, though considerably more street-wise.

The instigating event of the story is soon introduced and measures are taken. Mac informs everyone that the Growers' Association in Torgas Valley "just announced a pay cut to the pickers." He offers to head to the location and help organize a strike, suggesting that Jim join him for the experience.

The following morning, Jim and Mac hop a railroad car headed toward the valley. On their journey, Mac makes an instant impression on Jim, as he demonstrates his crafty handling of some belligerent travelers. Mac also takes this opportunity to discuss some useful habits, like smoking cigarettes, that help gain the trust and support of the working class.

Once in town, Mac leads them into a twenty-four-hour diner, where they receive a free meal from a party sympathizer named Al Anderson. Al proves to be a valuable resource in the effort to get the strike off the ground. Al informs Mac and Jim where the pickers congregate.

When Mac and Jim arrive at the gathering of pickers, they quickly realize that the leader of the group, a guy named London, has a daughter-in-law who is in the process of giving birth. Mac uses his general savvy to assist in the delivery of the baby and he subsequently gains London's trust.

The following day, as Mac had hoped, the news of their assistance travels through the grapevine and virtually every worker is aware of how Mac and Jim had assisted their leader. Mac and Jim take this opportunity to work among the people, picking fruit and instigating conversation about the wage cut. Jim spends the majority of the afternoon speaking with an older man named Dan, who responds to him with an admirable fire.

By lunch time, Mac and Jim meet up again, and Mac emphasizes the importance of acting quickly, before the pickers lose their drive. Mac tells Jim of the talk he had with London, who told him about a person named Dakin that could rally a group of pickers from the other end of the orchards.

That evening, London, Mac, and Jim set out to Dakin's place to speak with him about organizing a strike. Dakin is skeptical until Jim offers a timely insight about the possibility that the wage cut could carry over to the next job, unless the workers take action. Dakin agrees to discuss matters with his fellow workers.

The following day, while hauling in a bucket of apples, the checker confronts Jim and asks if he would relay information about the possibility of a strike, offering to compensate him for any information that would benefit the owners. During their lunch break, Jim tells Mac about the ironic incident. Mac emphasizes the importance of mingling with as many pickers as possible to gain a more accurate sense of their feelings toward a strike. As Jim converses with the workers, it becomes fairly apparent that a number have adopted a radical perspective. Eventually, Jim works his way back to Dan, the older man with whom he talked the previous day, and starts up another conversation. He manages to get Dan well heated up; Dan hops down on a ladder step, which breaks beneath his feet and sends him crashing to the ground. The workers rally around him, using the defective ladder and Dan's injury as the spark to instigate the strike.

Mac and Jim work quickly to organize the workers. Mac encourages Sam, one of London's most dedicated friends, to nominate London as chairman. While the workers are being organized, Mac and Jim head off to Al's lunch wagon to see if they can camp on his father's land. Al takes them to his father and allows Mac to use his powers of persuasion to convince Mr. Anderson into lending them his land. When Mr. Anderson has agreed, Mac and Jim head back to the orchard to check on the progress of the strike.

Upon their return, London tells them that the official word of the strike has been given to the super. The super has made it clear they are to leave the orchard property soon after sunrise. The next morning, Dick arrives with Doc Burton, the doctor whom Mac requested to oversee health standards at the Anderson camp.

Upon Mac's suggestion, London appoints group leaders to help organize the workers. They set up camp on the Anderson property and prepare to meet the scab workers who will be arriving by train the following day.

After settling into the Anderson camp, the strikers gather together and parade through town, under the close surveillance of the local police, and prepare to meet the incoming train. When it arrives, Joy emerges from the train and starts sending scabs into the line of strikers. When he steps away from the tracks, he is shot by a vigilante stationed in a nearby building.

Mac makes it clear that the strikers must use Joy's murder to elevate their level of emotion. Although Dakin views Mac as cold and heartless, he agrees that the men should rally behind Joy's death. When they arrive back at the camp, Anderson greets Mac brutishly and informs him that Al's lunch wagon has been burnt down and Al has been beaten up.

Later in the afternoon, Jim, Sam, and some other men picket a nearby orchard. In the process of trying to convert the scab workers, a fight breaks out and the strikers end up beating a group of scabs to the ground. Someone attacks them with gunfire and as they run, Jim gets shot through the shoulder.

Here the strike takes a difficult turn; the food supply is dwindling, spirits are low, and even Mac is beginning to have doubts. Dick arrives and tells everyone that the newspaper has run a false headline claiming that the supervisors were feeding them, thus making support from sympathizers more difficult to obtain. To make matters worse, the weather turns sour and it starts to rain.

Mac rises before sunrise and gets the men working on a stage for Joy's funeral; a funeral, he hopes, will get the strikers rallied up again. They eat the limited amount of grains they have left for breakfast and commence with the funeral. Meanwhile, the city officials have sent undercover spies to break up the men and create interior conflict. The funeral proves to be a necessary means of motivation for the men. London tries to speak to them but eventually turns the stage over to Mac, who drives them into an energized state.

Later that morning, the strikers parade into town, following the truck that is hauling Joy's coffin. While in town, they receive word that Dick has located a sympathizer willing to sacrifice two cows, a calf, and a barrel of beans for the striking men. Following the parade, Jim and Mac pick up the food and bring it back to camp. That night, everyone eats well and their vigor is temporarily renewed.

After the feast, Doc heads over to the Anderson house to check on Al. Shortly after, the barn catches on fire. It turns out that some vigilantes had lured the guards away from the house and set the barn on fire, destroying the entire apple crop that had been stored inside. In a fit of fury, Mr. Anderson vows to kick everyone off his property.

Reacting to the turn of events, Sam suggests that they burn down one of the wealthy landowners' houses. Mac, who had always remained rational in times of intensity, now gives in to his anger and encourages Sam to take action. This represents the turning point in Mac's relationship with Jim; up until now Jim had been resigned to being a voice in the background. Jim begins to believe that he is stronger, more rational, and more fit to lead. Mac eventually concedes to him.

Later in the evening, a stream of black smoke appears in the distance, indicating that Sam was successful in burning down a landowner's home. Mac sneaks into town late that night to mail a letter for supplies and see if he can pick up on any news. He returns just before dawn carrying a newspaper with the headline: "Strikers Burn Houses—Kill Men!" The article focuses on the communist agitators who are behind the entire strike.

As the morning breaks, they decide to picket in their trucks, anticipating that they will be met by swarms of officials. The men pile in the trucks and head off toward town. Before long they are back at camp, having been driven back by tear gas and machine guns. The strikers' spirits reach a new low.

Amidst the confusion and sense of hopelessness, one of the squad leaders, Burke, accuses London of selling them out. London reacts violently, striking Burke so forcefully that his jaw nearly comes off. In the momentum of the moment, urged on by Jim, London rallies the troops for a final time and leads them, as one forceful unit, back toward the barricade and through the barrage of guns and tear gas. Steinbeck uses this moment to highlight the theme of power within unity.

The final sequence of scenes begins as the men return from their march. Jim and Mac head up to the Anderson place to confirm that Al's father has filed a complaint to get them kicked off the land. When this is confirmed, they give Al permission to side with his father to prevent any further turmoil between them. Meanwhile the strikers have gathered on their own, without consulting London, Mac, or Jim. They decide they should take a final vote to decide whether it would be best to end the strike. Mac gives Jim the go ahead to act as the key note speaker at the meeting. At this point, with Al prepared to take the next step in his evolution as a party member, a young boy runs into the tent and tells them that the doctor, who had been missing for the past few days, is screaming for them from the orchard. Mac and Jim respond to the boy and head out into the orchard, where they realize quickly that they have been set up. Before they can react, Jim is shot dead. The novel ends as Mac carries Jim's body to the stage, lays him down, and exclaims that Jim "didn't want nothing for himself."

Steinbeck himself admitted that *In Dubious Battle* is a brutal story. In it, he presents violent events with a matter-of-fact tone that contains little warmth. However, the book's success lies in the fact that the characters are so real and believable that the reader is pulled into their story. ❀

List of Characters in
In Dubious Battle

Jim Nolan is the first character the reader encounters. His hunger for something to believe in leads him to join the Communist Party. Due to a wounded shoulder, he is committed to aiding the movement with his mind more than his body. He is preparing to take on the central leadership role when he is shot to death in the final scene of the novel.

Mac acts as the primary instigator and Jim's mentor throughout the novel. His savvy allows the strike to stay on its feet for as long as it does. He carries Jim's body and places it on the stage built for Joy's funeral in the final moment of the novel.

Harry Nilson is the Communist Party member with whom Jim speaks about becoming an active member. He introduces Jim to Mac and the rest of the field workers.

Dick is the dedicated party member who is able to find food and supplies for the strikers.

London is the leader of the strikers. He has the most contact with Jim and Mac, and ultimately plans on becoming an official member of the party following the strike. He is responsible for leading the final march into town.

Burke is the striker that accuses London of selling out; this incident leads London to break his jaw and instigates the final march through the barricade of tear gas and guns.

Doc Burton is the doctor responsible for maintaining health standards at the strikers' camp. His lack of commitment to the strikers' cause, but complete dedication toward his duty, makes him a sophisticated and engaging character.

Joy is the eccentric party member whose complete commitment to the cause leads to his insanity and finally his death.

Sam is London's most valued compatriot. He is responsible for burning down a landowner's home in retaliation for the burning of the Andersons' barn.

Dakin is responsible for rallying pickers to strike. He is sent to prison after reacting to the demolition of his prized truck.

Lisa is London's daughter-in-law who gives birth in the beginning of the novel. She and Jim form a bond throughout the latter portion of the novel.

Al Anderson is the owner of the lunch wagon where Jim and Mac stop for food upon first entering town. His father provides the land for the strikers to camp on. Al's lunch wagon gets burnt down and Al gets beaten up.

Mr. Anderson is Al's father who provides the land where the strikers camp. When his barn gets burnt down, he kicks the strikers out.

Dan is the old man whose fall from an orchard ladder touches off the strike. ✿

Critical Views on
In Dubious Battle

WARREN FRENCH ON NATURALISM AND
THE NOVEL'S CHARACTERS

[Warren French was a professor of English at Indiana University and Purdue University. His works include *The Social Novel at the End of an Era* and studies of Frank Norris and J. D. Salinger. In this excerpt, French discusses the "naturalistic" behavior in *In Dubious Battle*.]

The leading characters of *In Dubious Battle* are, like paisanos, social outsiders, though not even so sharp-witted. What differentiates Mac and Jim, two "red" labor organizers, from Steinbeck's earlier characters is their dedication to a "cause." They are spurred into action by their commitment to a vision of life, so that they are not, like Danny, victims of an unidentifiable force that intervenes between them and the achievement of a perfect harmony with life, but rather of a particular program to which they commit themselves without fully grasping the implications of such commitment. They differ (like George in *Of Mice and Men*) from the Munroes and Danny in being moved by a vision that transcends their own selfish ego; Steinbeck is beginning to move painfully— not very hopefully—toward the selfless vision of *The Grapes of Wrath*.

"We've a job to do," Mac tells Doc Burton in *In Dubious Battle*. "We've got no time to mess around with high-falutin' ideas." "Yes," Burton replies, "and so you start your work not knowing your medium. And your ignorance trips you up every time."

No exchange could better sum up the situation of the characters I describe as "naturalistic." Although this most pessimistic of Steinbeck's works portrays a strike in the Torgas Valley apple orchards of California, it focuses upon the brief career as a Communist activist of Jim Nolan. Sent out to assist a veteran organizer, he discovers at last a meaning in life; but tricked by vigilantes seeking to break the strike, he is lured to his death in an ambush.

Doc Burton tells the surviving partner:

"You practical men always lead practical men with stomachs. And something always gets out of hand. Your men get out of hand, they don't follow the rules of common sense, and you practical men either deny that it is so, or refuse to think about it. And when someone wonders what it is that makes a man with a stomach something more than your rule allows, why you howl, 'Dreamer, mystic, metaphysician!' . . . In all history there are no men who have come to such wild-eyed confusion and bewilderment as practical men leading men with stomachs."

Burton, of course, is striving for as complete self-consciousness as possible; and if he were to prevail, the novel might have turned into a drama of consciousness offering the final flickering of hope that *The Grapes of Wrath* does. But in this most pessimistic of Steinbeck's novels, the consciously thoughtful man is doomed as surely as those who are incapable of examining their commitments. On his way to visit a wounded man one night, the doctor simply disappears. There is no survival even for the man of good will in the "naturalistic" world of oaths and walking sticks.

—Warren French, "John Steinbeck: A Usable Concept of Naturalism." In *American Literary Naturalism: A Reassessment*, ed. Yoshinobu Hakutani and Fred Lewis (Heidelberg: Carl Winter Universitats Verlag, 1975): pp. 131–132.

JOHN H. TIMMERMAN ON THE NOVEL'S HISTORICAL BACKGROUND

[John H. Timmerman is professor of English at Calvin College in Grand Rapids, Michigan. His works include *The Dramatic Landscape of Steinbeck's Short Stories, John Steinbeck's Fiction: The Aesthetics of the Road Taken,* as well as numerous short stories, poems, and critical articles. In this excerpt, Timmerman refers to an essay on the background of *In Dubious Battle* by Jackson Benson and Anne Loftis, and discusses Steinbeck's use of fact in his fiction.]

Other details of a fascinating historical background are provided by Benson and Loftis, some parallels to the novel and some differences. Finally they poise us on the thin line between fact and fiction. In early reviews *In Dubious Battle* was proclaimed as "a straight story" of real human events and as "one of the most courageous and desperately honest books that has appeared in a long time." And in early criticism *In Dubious Battle* was proclaimed to be a story about "perversion of justice in the interest of owners, destruction of property and life, danger of violent revolution." The focus of attention lay decidedly in the historical accounting of the novel. In fact, the historical background did profoundly affect Steinbeck, and he steeped himself in it; but then he put it in the subconscious background as he crafted a wholly new—if parallel—world in his novel.

But if he was not content merely to give a historical rendition, if he was in fact "rearranging" an artistic perception of reality into a new artistic work, what was it that Steinbeck was creating in *In Dubious Battle*? What motivated and guided his rearrangement in the production of an artistic work? There are two responses to the question. The first lies in Steinbeck's exploration of what he called the Phalanx, the mob psychology of humanity. And this raises additional questions: Are human beings merely animals working collectively in one large organism? The answer is that humans can be but that they are not necessarily so. And that answer leads to the second fundamental response: the small struggles to achieve human dreams and establish human freedom in the quasi-Miltonic hell that is modern life. Benson and Loftis consider the final point:

> We cannot fault Steinbeck for being convincing, nor can we blame him for having chosen from his sources what he wished for his own purposes. The trouble lies in our persistent tendency to view the novel on our own, usually political and journalistic, terms. There is a darkness in this book that is pervasive. It runs from dark nights of confusion and muttering nightmares, to sullen, cloudy days of rain-soaked mobs, to dimly lit tents and their whispered conspiracies, into the souls of the bitter, suspicious men. This may not be Milton's hell, but it is certainly hell, nevertheless. That this depiction of hell, this parable of man's self-hatred, should still be thought of as one of our most journalistically truthful novels is an ironic comment on

our times, our taste, and the relationship of our literature
to our historical perceptions.

—John H. Timmerman, *John Steinbeck's Fiction: The Aesthetics of the Road Taken* (Norman, OK: University of Oklahoma Press, 1986): pp. 82–83.

LOUIS OWENS ON MAN AND BELONGING

[Louis Owens is a Professor of Literature at the University
of California at Santa Cruz. His works include: *John Steinbeck's Re-Vision of America* and *"The Grapes of Wrath":
Trouble in the Promised Land.* In this excerpt, Owens discusses social realism in *In Dubious Battle.*]

As every alert reader soon discovers, the plot of *In Dubious Battle*
turns upon a rather heavy irony. Jim Nolan, lonely and cut off as the
novel opens, grows in the course of the story to feel an overpowering
sense of belonging to the "cause." However, while Jim is moving
closer to this euphoric sense of belonging to something larger than
himself, he is becoming progressively dehumanized.

This level of irony functions, in part, to isolate the single impulse
upon which Steinbeck wished to focus: man's need to belong to
something larger than the isolated self, even if that something is as
dubious as the cause depicted in the novel. It is the belonging, pure
and simple, that brings Jim happiness. It is most clearly not whatever
good Jim is doing or may do for his fellow man.

Steinbeck explained his own interest in this novel in an oft-quoted
letter to George Albee: "I have used a small strike in an orchard
valley as the symbol of man's eternal, bitter warfare with himself. I'm
not interested in strike as means of raising men's wages, and I'm not
interested in ranting about justice and oppression, mere outcroppings which indicate the condition. But man hates something in
himself. He has been able to defeat every natural obstacle but himself he cannot win over unless he kills every individual. And this self-
hate which goes so closely in hand with self-love is what I wrote
about." Steinbeck went on in this same letter to say, "I wanted to be

merely a recording consciousness, judging nothing, simply putting down the thing."

Thus, although Steinbeck admitted that he had initially planned "to write a journalistic account of a strike," his ultimate interest in this novel was not social realism but rather an attempt to find what he, in another letter discussing "group man," called "a fictional symbolism which will act as a vehicle." Steinbeck's disinterest in social realism is further attested to by his statement to Carl Wilhelmson in August 1933: "I don't think you will like my latest work. It leaves realism farther and farther behind. I never had much ability for nor faith nor belief in realism." In another letter to Wilhelmson, dated April 1936 and referring to the just-published *In Dubious Battle*, Steinbeck again dismissed realism and said, "The Battle with its tricks to make a semblance of reality wasn't very close."

> —Louis Owens, "Writing 'In Costume': The Missing Voices of *In Dubious Battle*." In *John Steinbeck: The Years of Greatness, 1936–1939*, ed. Tetsumaro Hayashi (Tuscaloosa, AL: University of Alabama Press, 1993): pp. 80–82.

ABBY H. P. WERLOCK ON JIM NOLAN'S MOTHER

[Abby H. P. Werlock is a professor of American Literature at St. Olaf College in Minnesota. She has published articles and reviews on Cooper, Faulkner, Hemingway, Steinbeck, Twain, and Wharton. In this excerpt, Werlock discusses the effect of Jim's mother on his development.]

Within the first few pages of the novel, as Jim speaks of feeling "dead," he tells a stranger, the Communist party man Harry Nilson, his family history. Both his parents are deceased, and his father, Roy Nolan, was well known for his violent propensities, which eventually resulted in his death—from a charge of buckshot in the chest— during an arson attempt. Jim seems to have inherited his anger and his temper from his father, but as Mac points out, Jim's old man knew only how to "fight": "I don't know where you learned to use your bean and keep clear," he says, and Jim replies that his intelligence and ability to reason derive from his mother.

Although Mrs. Nolan is given no name, she acquires stature, not only because Jim continually recalls her, but also because she is the only character in the novel who professes any religious beliefs—and Jim seems to have inherited her spiritual tendencies as well. Memories of his mother frame the novel. At the beginning he tells Nilson that his mother was a Catholic, but his "old man wouldn't let her go to church. He hated churches." Only at the end, with the growing friendship of Jim and Lisa, do we comprehend the full force of the feminine in his life. Just before his own death Jim tells the rest of the story: sometimes his mother would take him to church in the middle of the week—even though his father would have been furious had he known of these religious pilgrimages—and Jim felt peaceful when looking at the statue of Mary the Mother.

Jim never seems to mourn his father's death, but he speaks of his mother's several times. Notably, he joins the Communist party, not after his father's death, but almost immediately after his mother's; part of his spirit seems to have departed with her. At her death he has lost both women in his life, and he tells their stories. When he was still a boy, his older sister, May, suddenly vanished one day. She was fourteen, a pretty girl with yellow hair. Despite police questionings of her schoolgirl friends, the mystery of her disappearance remains unsolved, but the clear implication is that she was abducted. From that point on his mother, whose light-blue eyes become like "white stones," with "a kind of dead look," is miserable, voiceless, silenced, "quieter even than before."

—Abby H. P. Werlock, "Looking at Lisa: The Function of the Feminine in Steinbeck's *In Dubious Battle.*" In *John Steinbeck: The Years of Greatness, 1936–1939*, ed. Tetsumaro Hayashi (Tuscaloosa, AL: University of Alabama Press, 1993): pp. 49–50.

[Jay Parini is a professor of English at Middlebury College in Vermont. His works include *Anthracite County* and *The Patch Boys*. In this excerpt, Parini talks on the use of myth in Steinbeck's fiction.]

The characters in this drama are locked, as the line from *Paradise Lost* suggests, "In dubious battle on the plains of heaven." Critics have drawn the appropriate parallels between Milton's epic and Steinbeck's novel, seeing the Party as Satan (red is the Devil's color), with London serving as Beelzebub, Satan's right-hand man. Dick, the "bedroom radical," is Belial, and so forth. The debates about how to proceed against "the authorities" echo similar debates among the fallen angels of Milton's epic.

The Christ symbolism seen in *To a God Unknown* is present again in this novel, too obviously so, with Jim Nolan standing in as Jesus, the figure who appears from nowhere with a passion for the outcast and downtrodden; he ultimately sacrifices himself—quite literally— for the sake of "his people." Steinbeck reinforces these associations in several ways: near the end of Chapter 13 one hears roosters crowing; when Jim is suffering from his wound, he asks for water; in the last chapter we are told that Nolan's "face was transfigured. A furious light of energy seemed to shine from it." And after Nolan's murder, Mac says of him: "This guy didn't want nothing for himself," emphasizing his Christlike nature.

Typically, Steinbeck multiplies the levels of mythical reference, a technique that, in this novel, seems rather crude. Warren French, however, admires the novel's texture and sees the Arthurian legend emerging once more; he notes "a remarkable psychological similarity between Jim Nolan, the central character of the novel, and one of the principal knights of the Round Table, Perceval or Parsifal as he is best known. . . ." Nolan is "a modern exemplar of the chivalric ideals of adventurousness (he longs for action and is finally killed by his impetuousness), selflessness, and chastity."

Steinbeck uses myth in a familiar way to organize his ideas and ground his work in archetypal patterns, while never losing sight of the need to summon a reality that is fresh and concrete. Evoking the lives of its characters in all their gritty particularity, the novel moves beyond a study of social unrest and the oppression of the poor to the contemplation of what one critic, Julian N. Hartt, has called "eschatological man." Hartt suggests that *In Dubious Battle* "deals seriously with eschatological man. Eschatological man so imaged is a creature with a terrible duality of motivations: violent resentment of the social forces which have cheated him out of his rights; and passionate attachment to a splendid vision of an age to come when the furious conflict generated by injustice will have been resolved forever into the peace of a classless community."

One senses this duality of attachments in Steinbeck himself. He had a peculiar and noble sympathy for those who were cheated out of their natural birthright and dignity. Injustice drove him wild; as his sister Beth says, "Even as a child John sided with the underdog." These radical or, more precisely, liberal sympathies bound him, psychologically, to the present struggle, whatever it might be; on the other hand, his philosophical and spiritual drive led him to posit a utopian moment, "the peace of a classless community." All progressive politics depend on this duality, and Steinbeck (in his most activist period) seems to have drawn great energies from this unusually generative conflict.

—Jay Parini, *John Steinbeck: A Biography* (New York: Henry Holt, 1995): pp. 167–168.

BRIAN E. RAILSBACK ON MOTIVATION OF THE NOVEL'S CHARACTERS

[Brian E. Railsback is the director of writing and editing at Western Carolina University. His works include *Parallel Expeditions: Charles Darwin and the Art of John Steinbeck.* In this excerpt, Railsback discusses Steinbeck's interest in human self-hatred and the violence of *In Dubious Battle*.]

In Dubious Battle is a perfect illustration of Steinbeck's phalanx theory, that idea of which Steinbeck told friend George Albee in a 1933 letter, "There is a life time of work in it and strangely enough it is directly in line with the whole process of my other work." As Steinbeck well knew, the novel is not a simple strike novel or proletarian tract—the political implications were not that important to him. "I'm not interested in strike as means of raising men's wages," Steinbeck writes of his novel to Albee in 1935, "and I'm not interested in ranting about justice and oppression, mere outcroppings which indicate the condition." What interests him is the human self-hatred: "But man hates something in himself. He has been able to defeat every natural obstacle but himself he cannot win over unless he kills every individual. . . . The book is brutal." Indeed, the novel dramatizes a species' competition with itself, the battling phalanxes of a superior fighting animal meet over the same lush territory to destroy each other. The struggle for survival is the substructure of what appears to be an ideological battle between capitalism and communism, the "mere outcroppings" of something deeper and ancient. Steinbeck's idea has interesting implications for his view of *Homo sapiens*; it puts an eerie light on such endless wars as we find in Bosnia, Ireland, and the Middle East.

From the neon restaurant sign "exploding its hard red light" in the second sentence of the novel to the abrupt cutting off of the final sentence during the speech over Jim Nolan's mutilated body, *In Dubious Battle* is thoroughly violent. As Betty Perez has shown, several critics have seen the novel as unnecessarily violent. It is a brutal portrayal of human self-hate, the fearsome physical struggle of man against man. In a world of beaten and crushed people, such as Jim's father or the hapless Joy, even a simple greeting resonates with violence, a sizing up of potential opponents. This uneasiness is apparent when Jim meets Mac for the first time: "Too bad we're not dogs, we could get that all over with," Mac tells Jim as they inspect each other, "We'd either be friends or fighting by now." Mac decides to apprentice Jim as a strike organizer, "Kind of like teaching hunting dogs by running them with the old boys, see."

Mac's dog/man similes make sense, for the characters in the novel act on an elemental level. For a strike novel, there is very little emphasis on ideology, just as Steinbeck planned: "I guess it is a brutal book, more brutal because there is no author's moral point of view." In a letter to his agent, Mavis McIntosh, Steinbeck responds to some criticism from his publisher, Pat Covici: "Answering the complaint that the ideology is incorrect, this is the silliest of criticism. . . . [I]deologies change to fit a situation. . . . In any statement by one of the protagonists I have simply used statements I have heard used." With such a view of ideologies, coupled with the desire to display *Homo sapiens* in competition with itself, no wonder the proletarian comments have small importance in the book. They are not speeches Steinbeck worked over, but fragmented recordings of things he heard tossed off. This viewpoint is reinforced by Doc Burton (one of Steinbeck's characterizations of Ed Ricketts). Doc observes that "when group-man wants to move he makes a standard. 'God wills that we recapture the Holy Land': or he says, 'We fight to make the world safe for democracy': or he says, 'We will wipe out social injustice with communism.'" Even Mac does not believe all the rhetoric he feeds the men, telling Jim that they have no chance of winning the strike for which the strikers will kill and die, even adding, "[I]f we won, Jim, if we put it over, our own side would kill us. I wonder why we do it." Except for some vague notions that the strike may lead to better things in the future, not even Mac can clearly explain its purpose. So much for the importance of ideological movements—Steinbeck wants to cut through politics and see what truly causes people to fight and kill each other.

—Brian E. Railsback, *Parallel Expeditions: Charles Darwin and the Art of John Steinbeck* (Moscow, ID: University of Idaho Press, 1995): pp. 70–71.

ROBERT DEMOTT ON CALIFORNIA

[Robert Demott is a professor of English at Ohio University in Athens, Ohio. His works include *Steinbeck's Readings: A Catalogue of Books Owned and Borrowed*, *After "The Grapes of Wrath": Essays on John Steinbeck in Honor of Tetsumaro Hayashi*, and *Steinbeck's Typewriter: Essays on His Art*. He has edited many anthologies of Steinbeck's work, including *Working Days: The Journal of "The Grapes of Wrath," 1938–1941* and *John Steinbeck: Novels and Stories, 1932–1937*. This excerpt discusses California and Steinbeck's fiction.]

My first inkling that conditions might actually be different in California came when I hit this passage in "Flight," one of the powerful stories in Steinbeck's collection *The Long Valley*: "Below him lay a deep canyon exactly like the last, waterless and desolate. There was no flat, no oak trees, not even heavy brush in the bottom of it. And on the other side a sharp ridge stood up, thinly brushed with starving sage, littered with broken granite. Strewn over the hill there were giant outcroppings, and on the top the granite teeth stood out against the sky." This sounded more like hell than heaven, more like a nether land than nirvana. My cherished view of California as a balmy tropical paradise took a sharp turn; further beatings came in rapid succession when I encountered the drought in *To a God Unknown*, the ominous fog (a condition I believed indigenous to New England) which hangs like a lid over Elisa Allen in "The Chrysanthemums," the brutality of the orchard strike in *In Dubious Battle*, and Lennie Small's sacrificial murder in *Of Mice and Men*. (Where, I asked myself, did the concept of the "whole" man with its ethically upright posture, its yearning toward radiance, harmony, and goodness, fit into these novels? I wished some of my professors had leavened their Aquinas with Steinbeck.) Clearly, California was another country; apparently, as a friend of mine said, they did things differently there. (Years later, when I set foot in California for the first time, my reading of Steinbeck, which by then had become extensive, helped ease but did not eliminate my sense of culture shock. I could never shake the feeling that I was in a foreign country, and I began to sense that Steinbeck's paranoia was accurate when he said that actions that were tolerated elsewhere in the United States were probably crimes in California.)

But such rude awakenings aside, Steinbeck's unpretentiousness, his accessibility, struck me as thoroughly refreshing. I loved the way his weird, crazy characters, like The Seer in *To a God Unknown*, never quite fit into a blueprint and the way his serious ones too, like Doc Burton in *In Dubious Battle*, always probed the axis of reality with their questionings. They were just the opposite of the ethereal protagonists I was reading about in my class on British fiction. For the first time in my life literature seemed recognizably "real." Steinbeck's characters reminded me of members of my own kin: the kindness of Billy Buck, the obsessiveness of Joseph Wayne, the chicanery of Danny, the hunger of Peter Randall, the frustration of Elisa Allen. In Steinbeck's family portraits I recognized all the positive gestures as well as the grotesqueries, willful rationalizations, and psychological quirks because they were my own, or belonged to members of my own blood—this aunt, that uncle, those cousins; the more I read, the more I began to think of his work in terms of similarities rather than differences only, in terms of a family beyond the family I already possessed.

—Robert Demott, *Steinbeck's Typewriter: Essays on His Art* (Troy, NY: Whitson, 1996): pp. 272–273.

James C. Kelley on Steinbeck's Concept of Phalanx

[James C. Kelley is the dean of science and engineering at San Francisco State University. His works include numerous articles on the productivity of the nearshore environment. In this excerpt, Kelley discusses the phalanx concept in *In Dubious Battle*.]

In another form, visceral understanding may be manifested in group behavior of animals and humans, when, as Ed says in the above lines from "The Tide," "whole collections of animals act as one individual responding to a natural phenomenon." This idea of course pervades Steinbeck's novels and has been explored at length by Richard Astro (1973), where John's formulation is the phalanx concept.

A theme central to the phalanx concept is the notion that the collection of individuals in an ecosystem, a group, or as a superorganism, like a person drinking alcohol, may even exhibit behaviors that are inimical to the survival of individual components (e.g., brain cells) of the system. In *In Dubious Battle* Doc Burton says, "The pleasure we get in scratching an itch causes death to a great number of cells. Maybe group-man gets pleasure when individual men are wiped out in a war." When Joy and Jim die, Mac turns the events into energy for the superorganism. "I want to see if it'd be a good idea for the guys to look at him tomorrow. We got to shoot some juice into 'er some way. . . . If Joy can do some work after he's dead, then he's got to do it. There's no such things as personal feelings in this crowd."

The phalanx concept was one that had interested John for some time, but it certainly took shape and developed substance from his conversations with Ed Ricketts. As John wrote to George Albee in 1933,

> *I can't give you the whole thing [the phalanx concept] com-*
> *pletely in a letter, George. I am going to write a whole novel*
> *with it as a theme, so how can I get it in a letter? Ed Ricketts*
> *has dug up all the scientific material and more than I need to*
> *establish the physical integrity of the thing. I have written the*
> *theme over and over and did not know what I was writing, I*
> *found at least four statements of it in the God. . . .When your*
> *phalanx needs you it will use you, if you are the material to*
> *be used. You will know when the time comes, and when it*
> *does come, nothing you can do will let you escape.*

—James C. Kelley, "John Steinbeck and Ed Ricketts: Understanding Life in the Great Tide Pool." In *Steinbeck and the Environment: Interdisciplinary Approaches*, ed. Susan F. Beegel, Susan Shillinglaw and Wesley N. Tiffney, Jr. (Tuscaloosa, AL: University of Alabama Press, 1997): pp. 36–37.

Plot Summary of
Of Mice and Men

Of Mice and Men speaks of human loneliness against the panorama of nature. The book reveals Steinbeck's feelings about the natural world, for the story is full of Steinbeck's careful observations of humanity's place in the natural environment. It describes the human longing to find a home within nature, a place the story equates with the "fat of the land."

The story opens along the Salinas river, as George Milton, a small, serious man, walks with his traveling companion Lennie Small, an enormous, mentally-challenged man, toward the farm where they have been hired to buck barley. Their plan is to find a spot to sleep beside the river and then travel on to the farm in the morning. While they walk, the reader is made aware of Lennie's fondness for soft textures, particularly furry animals. This fondness leads Lennie to pick up a dead mouse from the road and store it in his pocket until George demands that he throw it away. George goes on to say, as he has done on numerous occasions, that he could be doing a great deal better for himself if he didn't have to take care of Lennie. This speech leads into a more sentimental monologue about friendship and the dream of one day owning a plot of land where they can farm and herd animals and own rabbits, which Lennie can take care of. They are a team, and as a team, they look out for one another.

The following day, upon arriving at the bunk house, George makes it clear that Lennie is not to speak under any circumstances. The first person they encounter is an old man named Candy and his old sheep dog. Soon after, the boss acknowledges their arrival and reprimands them for not showing up in the morning. They also meet Curley, the boss's spiteful son, who immediately dislikes Lennie. When they leave, Candy claims that Curley feels threatened by any one with height, indicating that he has a complex about his size. George recognizes that Curley could cause trouble for them and insists that Lennie avoid him at all costs.

Not long after Curley leaves, George and Lennie meet Slim, a charismatic field worker, and Curley's wife, an attractive, flirtatious woman who seems to be on a perpetual quest to draw people's attention. Lennie is noticeably impressed by her appearance, a fact that makes George increasingly edgy. They are also introduced to a large laborer named Carlson, who has a fondness for guns. Carlson is disgusted by Candy's old dog, which he claims stinks up the entire bunk house. He suggests that Candy shoot his dog and take one of the puppies from Slim's dog's litter. Hearing that Slim has a litter of puppies, Lennie becomes excited. Without his asking, George knows that Lennie wants him to ask Slim about a puppy.

After eating lunch, George engages in conversation with Slim, who agrees to give one of his puppies to Lennie. In the conversation, George praises Lennie for being tremendously strong, a great worker, and despite his intellectual handicap, a person who follows instruction extremely well. George also tells Slim about an incident in Weed, the last town in which they worked, where Lennie tried to touch the material on a woman's dress, leading her to accuse Lennie of attempted rape. George emphasizes Lennie's good nature and insists that he would never hurt anything out of meanness.

That night, Carlson starts in again about Candy's dog, urging Candy to let him shoot it. Though it is clear that the dog means a great deal to Candy, Carlson's pressure is too much and Candy gives in. After Carlson takes the dog out back, Crooks, an African American man who works in the stable, informs Slim that he has heated the tar to secure the hoof on Slim's mule.

After Slim leaves with Crooks, only Lennie, George, and Candy remain in the room. With Lennie's encouragement, George begins to speak about the farm house that they hope to buy, and the chickens and vegetables and rabbits they will have. He continues to elaborate about the land and the food and the lifestyle they'll lead. As he speaks, Candy, who has been facing the wall in a state of despair, turns around and asks them about the farm. At first, George responds defensively, having scarcely even realized that Candy was in the room, but once the old man expresses a genuine interest in the logistics and offers to contribute a sum of money he has been saving, George goes right back to describing their dream.

The conversation is interrupted by the entrance of Slim, Curley, and another worker, Whit. Slim is upset with Curley, who accused him of making advances toward his wife. As their heated exchange continues, Curley notices Lennie, who is still smiling about the prospect of owning rabbits, and approaches him aggressively, demanding that he disclose the reason for his smile. Curley backs Lennie into the wall and strikes him repeatedly in the face and torso. As Lennie cowers against the wall, screaming for help, George orders him to defend himself. After a few more blows to his face and a few more demands from George to "Get 'em," Lennie catches Curley's fist in his hand and crushes it, forcing Curley to the floor. The entire room stands in amazement at Lennie's incredible display of physical strength. When Lennie finally lets go of Curley's hand, Slim makes it clear that Curley will not get Lennie fired or else the word will spread that he was humiliated at Lennie's hands.

The action resumes later in the evening in Crooks' room, when Lennie appears at the door. Lennie tells Crooks that the rest of the guys went into town for women and drinks. Though Crooks initially seems bothered by Lennie's presence, he quickly welcomes him into his room, claiming that few people have ever been inside. Soon after Lennie settles into Crooks' room, Candy arrives and invites himself in. The conversation soon turns to the farm they are hoping to buy, a prospect that peeks Crooks' interest. Their conversation is interrupted by Curley's wife, who has come looking for Curley.

Crooks and Candy greet Curley's wife coldly, claiming that she likes to stir up trouble. She remains at the entrance of Crooks' room until the others return from town and everyone goes back to the bunk house.

The story resumes the following day as Lennie is in the barn, stroking the puppy he has accidentally killed with overzealous affection. As he considers the best way of dealing with the situation, a way which will not put his hopes of tending rabbits in jeopardy, Curley's wife enters the barn. Lennie talks with her for a while and mentions his fondness for soft objects. Curley's wife entices Lennie to touch her hair, which she claims is extraordinarily soft. Lennie begins stroking her hair, unconsciously getting more aggressive with his strokes. This causes Curley's wife to yell at Lennie and jerk her body, prompting him to squeeze her head and cover her mouth with his hand, begging that she not make noise. The struggling continues until Lennie, desperate to silence Curley's wife for fear she will ruin his chances at tending rabbits, shakes her body back and forth until her neck snaps. Lennie, realizing that he has done a "bad thing," flees from the barn and heads for the spot beside the river where George told him to go in case of trouble.

Candy is the first one to discover the body. He immediately finds George and the two decide to let Candy tell the others, so they don't blame George for what has occurred. When the others realize what has happened, Curley vows to hunt Lennie down and shoot him. After gathering a few guns together and realizing that Carlson's gun is missing, they head out to find Lennie.

The action concludes as George meets Lennie at the designated trouble spot. He is surprisingly calm and instead of giving him the "you are a burden" speech, George starts to tell Lennie about the farm they're going to buy and the life they're going to lead. He asks Lennie to look out over the water so he can visualize the scene in his mind. As George continues to recite the story, he raises Carlson's gun, which the others had suspected Lennie of stealing, and shoots Lennie in the back of the head. The novel ends as the others arrive and see what George has done. Only Slim seems to relate to George on a human level.

Throughout the story, Steinbeck's own compassion is clear. With his usual objective, non-sentimental style, he conveys his understanding of those who are downtrodden and below the average. The book is full of the loneliness of these people—Old Candy, who has only his dog; Crooks, who is willing to work for nothing if he can only have someone with whom to talk; Candy's wife, who apparently lacks even a name.

In contrast to this loneliness is the relationship between Lennie and George. Their dream for a better future is tied to their commitment to each other. Unfortunately, the two things—their friendship and their hope—are so tightly tied together that when one is destroyed, so is the other. ❈

List of Characters in
Of Mice and Men

George Milton is the small, serious man who travels with mentally handicapped companion Lennie Small and looks after him. George provides the direction and the dream which keeps them motivated. He shoots Lennie through the back of the head in the closing scene of the novel.

Lennie Small is the large, mentally-handicapped man who is George's loyal follower and friend. Lennie's uncontrollable impulses and ignorance of social standards continually get him in trouble. He is shot by George at the end of the novel, after inadvertently snapping Curley's wife's neck.

Candy is the old man who works at the bunk house and is the first person to find the body of Curley's wife.

Curley is the mean-spirited son of the boss. His hand gets crushed by Lennie and his wife is killed accidentally by Lennie.

Curley's wife is a flirtatious character who seems obsessed with drawing the attention of her husband's work mates. She is killed unintentionally by Lennie after she offers to let him stroke her soft hair.

Slim is the charismatic ranch hand who commands a great deal of respect among his fellow workers.

Crooks is the African American stable keeper who is forced to live in the barn. He and Lennie have a meaningful exchange the evening before the novel's final incident.

Carlson is the large field worker who insists that Candy let him shoot his old, decrepit dog. ❀

Critical Views on
Of Mice and Men

SAMUEL I. BELLMAN ON LENNY, CONTROL, AND FREEDOM

[Samuel I. Bellman has published scholarly essays for a variety of different journals, including an essay on Steinbeck for the *CEA Critic*, a journal of the College English Association. In this excerpt, Bellman speaks on Lennie and George as two parts of the Freudian mind: Lenny as id and George as ego.]

Applying this notion of Steinbeck's pessimistic energy-system scheme (things are running down, but *loss* will bring a kind of *replacement*) to *Of Mice and Men* reveals an interesting paradox having to do with freedom and control. First we will have to recap the story briefly, accenting certain psychological features. The scene is a ranch near Soledad, California, and the two chief characters are a pair of itinerant farm workers, George (the responsible one, who makes the decisions and lays the plans) and Lennie (the retarded and irresponsible one, whom George will always have to take care of). In a sense, George and Lennie are to each other as *ego* is to *id* in the same mind: the conscious, reality-sensitive regulator always having to keep in check the primitive, violent instincts.

The crux of this story about the best laid plans of mice and men often going awry is the dilemma George faces after Lennie accidentally kills the boss's daughter-in-law. The aroused ranch hands, led by Curley (the dead woman's husband) run out to find Lennie and shoot him. George, who has stolen a gun from one of the men, gets to Lennie first. The two have a heart-to-heart talk, reiterating (each on his own level) their hopes and problems. It is as though a human mind were having a dialogue with itself, matching one viewpoint with another or, let us say, *ego* with *id*. George feels he will have to kill Lennie to spare his being killed (and, we suspect, being worked over, first) by the others. But it is hard for George to pull the trigger and yet even harder for him not to, which would mean exposing Lennie to a brutal murder by the gang. Finally, after a real heart-to-heart talk, George manages to shoot the unsuspecting, eternally repentant and hopeful Lennie.

So suspenseful and yet painful is the conclusion to the tale that the reader may easily miss a number of peculiar implications. First, George was a "whole" person only so long as he was tied up to Lennie, looking out for him, denying himself all the pleasures of the senses so he could save his money and they could buy a place of their own. It was the unusual buddyship of the two, the story makes clear, that rendered possible a glorious dream of self-improvement, a constructive hope to live by. But their dream of a place of their own was shattered after Lennie killed the woman. The kind of self-improvement held up as an ideal in the story was possible neither through the buddyship of George and Lennie nor through George's going it alone.

Second, George came to feel that he had to kill Lennie for Lennie's own good. And with Lennie dead, George could raise all the hell he had wanted to before but had been prevented (ostensibly by Lennie) from doing. Third, Lennie, as an *id*-figure, had actually exercised a restraining, inhibiting effect on George: the effect of the super-ego, the restrictions of society. But with Lennie dead, George was apparently about to become an *id*-figure himself, giving free rein to his "lower" desires and impulses. However, there is one more implication that cannot be overlooked: the matter of Authority.

—Samuel I. Bellman, "Control and Freedom in Steinbeck's *Of Mice and Men*," *CEA Critic* 38, no. 1 (November 1975): pp. 25–26.

MICHAEL W. SHURGOT ON SYMBOLIC CARD GAMES

[Michael W. Shurgot has contributed scholarly essays to a variety of different journals including the *Steinbeck Quarterly*, which is devoted to study of the works of John Steinbeck. In this excerpt, Shurgot discusses themes of isolation in *Of Mice and Men*, illustrated by symbolic card games.]

George's card games are generally symbolic in three ways. Lester Jay Marks writes that Steinbeck's novel is "disciplined by his non-teleological methods of observing 'phenomena.' He is concerned not with the *why* but with the *what* and *how* of the individual's illusions." Steinbeck's original title, "Something That Happened," is, according to Marks, an unsentimental comment upon the "tragic reversal of fortunes" that George and Lennie experience. A non-teleological world is one of chance, of reversals of fortune beyond man's comprehension or his power to control. And a game of cards is an exact symbol of this kind of world. In card games there is no pattern to the cards' random appearance; their sequence is solely a matter of chance. Analogically, although George tries to control Lennies' activities and movements on the ranch, he cannot prevent Lennie's tragic meeting with Curley's wife in the barn.

Further, George's card game is solitaire. From the opening dialogue between George and Lennie, to the novel's final, terrifying moments, Steinbeck's characters talk about the isolation, rootlessness, and alienation of their lives. Steinbeck introduces the theme of isolation shortly after George and Lennie arrive at the clearing in part one. George laments,

> Guys like us, that work on ranches, are the loneliest guys in the world. They got no family. They don't belong no place. They come to a ranch an' work up a stake and then they go inta town and blow their stake, and the first thing you know they're poundin' their tail on some other ranch. They ain't got nothing to look ahead to.

George's sense of the loneliness and rootlessness of ranchhands is echoed several times in the novel. In section two, Slim observes, "Ain't many guys travel around together. . . . I don't know why. Maybe ever'body in the whole damn world is scared of each other." Early in section three, Slim elaborates on the uniqueness of George's relationship with Lennie:

> Funny how you an' him string along together. . . . I hardly never seen two guys travel together. You know how the hands are, they just come in and get their bunk and work a month, and then they quit and go out alone. Never seem to give a damn about nobody. It jus' seems kinda funny a cuckoo like him and a smart little guy like you travelin' together.

George tells Slim he "ain't got no people," and insists that, although Lennie is a "God damn nuisance most of the time," nonetheless traveling with him is preferable to the loneliness and misery of most ranchhands' lives:

> I seen the guys that go around on the ranches alone. That ain't no good. They don't have no fun. After a long time they get mean. They get wantin' to fight all the time.

Later, after George has told Candy about his and Lennie's dream of owning their own place, Candy, obviously enthralled at being included in their plans, says that he would leave his share of the place to them ". . . 'cause I ain't got no relatives nor nothing."

—Michael W. Shurgot, "A Game of Cards in Steinbeck's *Of Mice and Men*," *Steinbeck Quarterly* 15, no. 1/2 (Winter/Spring 1982): pp. 38–39.

LOUIS OWENS ON THE NOVEL'S EDEN MYTH

[Louis Owens is a Professor of Literature at the University of California at Santa Cruz. His works include: *John Steinbeck's Re-Vision of America* and *"The Grapes of Wrath": Trouble in the Promised Land,* as well as numerous articles, fiction, and creative nonfiction. In this excerpt, Owens discusses the Eden myth in *Of Mice and Men.*]

The Eden myth looms large in *Of Mice and Men* (1937), the play-novella set along the Salinas River "a few miles south of Soledad." And, as in all of Steinbeck's California fiction, setting plays a central role in determining the major themes of this work. The fact that the setting for *Of Mice and Men* is a California valley dictates, according to the symbolism of Steinbeck's landscapes, that this story will take place in a fallen world and that the quest for the illusive and illusory American Eden will be of central thematic significance. In no other work does Steinbeck demonstrate greater skill in merging the real setting of his native country with the thematic structure of his novel.

Critics have consistently recognized in Lennie's dream of living "off the fatta the lan'" on a little farm the American dream of a new

Eden. Joseph Fontenrose states concisely, "The central image is the earthly paradise. . . . It is a vision of Eden." Peter Lisca takes this perception further, noting that "the world of *Of Mice and Men* is a fallen one, inhabited by sons of Cain, forever exiled from Eden, the little farm of which they dream." There are no Edens in Steinbeck's writing, only illusions of Eden, and in the fallen world of the Salinas Valley—which Steinbeck would later place "east of Eden"—the Promised Land is an illusory and painful dream. In this land populated by "sons of Cain," men condemned to wander in solitude, the predominant theme is that of loneliness, or what Donald Pizer has called "fear of apartness." Pizer has, in fact, discovered the major theme of this novel when he says, "One of the themes of *Of Mice and Men* is that men fear loneliness, that they need someone to be with and to talk to who will offer understanding and companionship."

The setting Steinbeck chose for this story brilliantly underscores the theme of man's isolation and need for commitment. Soledad is a very real, dusty little town on the western edge of the Salinas River midway down the Salinas Valley. Like most of the settings in Steinbeck's fiction, this place exists; it *is*. However, with his acute sensitivity to place names and his knowledge of Spanish, Steinbeck was undoubtedly aware that "Soledad" translates into English as "solitude" or "loneliness." In this country of solitude and loneliness, George and Lennie stand out sharply because they have each other or, as George says, "We got somebody to talk to that gives a damn about us." Cain's question is the question again at the heart of this novel: "Am I my brother's keeper?" And the answer found in the relationship between George and Lennie is an unmistakable confirmation.

Of Mice and Men is most often read as one of Steinbeck's most pessimistic works, smacking of pessimistic determinism. Fontenrose suggests that the novel is about "the vanity of human wishes" and asserts that, more pessimistically than Burns, "Steinbeck reads, 'All schemes o' mice and men gang *ever* agely'" [my italics]. Howard Levant, in a very critical reading of the novel, concurs, declaring that "the central theme is stated and restated—the good life is impossible because humanity is flawed." In spite of the general critical reaction, and without disputing the contention that Steinbeck allows no serious hope that George and Lennie will ever achieve their dream farm, it is nonetheless possible to read *Of Mice and Men* in a more optimistic light than has been customary. In previous works we have seen a pattern established in which the Steinbeck hero achieves greatness in the midst of, even because of, apparent defeat. In *Of Mice and Men*, Steinbeck accepts, very non-teleologically, the fact that man is flawed and the Eden myth mere illusion. However, critics have consistently under-valued Steinbeck's emphasis on the theme of commitment, which runs through the novel and which is the chief ingredient in the creation of the Steinbeck hero.

—Louis Owens, *John Steinbeck's Re-Vision of America* (Athens, GA: University of Georgia Press, 1985): pp. 100–102.

ANNE LOFTIS ON THE CHARACTERS OF THE NOVEL

[Anne Loftis is a historian and freelance writer based in Menlo Park, California. Her works include *California, Where the Twain DID Meet*. In this excerpt, Loftis speaks on the setting of the novel and the roles various characters play in *Of Mice and Men*.]

The characters who come in one by one create the social dimension of the place. This rough lodging in which nothing has been provided beyond the bare necessities is governed by the harsh code of the men who live there for a week, a month, or a year. It is a society intolerant of weakness or difference. Old Candy, helpless to stop the shooting of his dog, knows that he too will be banished when he is no longer useful. Crooks, the black stable hand, is excluded except on Christmas when the boss brings in a gallon of whiskey for the entire crew. The rest of the year Crooks plays horseshoes outside with the others, but when they come indoors to sleep, he goes off alone to his bed in the harness room of the barn.

Women are not welcome in this male enclave. Curley's wife, wandering around the ranch in a wistful quest for some kind of human contact, is stereotyped by the men, whose experience of women comes from "old Suzy" and her girls in town. Curley's wife (in the novel she has no other name) goes along with the typecasting by playing the vamp, inflaming her jealous husband, who, as the son of the boss, is as powerful as he is vicious. It is on this explosive situation that the plot turns. Lennie, sensing trouble too complicated for a simple mind to unravel, begs to leave after George tells him that Curley's wife is "poison" and "jail bait."

Steinbeck had a different view of her, as he explained in a letter to the actress who played the role in the Broadway production of the play. Curley's wife acts seductively because "she knows instinctively that if she is to be noticed at all, it will be because someone finds her sexually attractive." But her pose is deceptive. "Her moral training was most rigid." She was a virgin until her marriage and had had no sexual experience outside her unfulfilling union with Curly. She had grown up "in an atmosphere of fighting and suspicion" and had "learned to be hard to cover her fright." But she is fundamentally "a nice, kind girl" who has "a natural trustfulness. . . . If anyone—a man or a woman—ever gave her a break—treated her like a person—she would be a slave to that person."

Steinbeck captured this aspect of her character in her final scene with Lennie. In the presence of this childlike man she drops her defenses and expresses her real feelings. Her rambling monologue of blighted hopes and tawdry fantasies is, in effect, a last confession.

Steinbeck has prepared his readers for the shocking climax of the novel through his portrait of Lennie. He might have created a caricature in the mental defective who crushes soft creatures in his powerful hands. He had worked with a real-life Lennie, he told reporters when he was writing the stage version of *Of Mice and Men*. "He didn't kill a girl. He killed a ranch foreman. Got sore because the boss had fired his pal and stuck a pitchfork right through his stomach." The fictional Lennie is passive and nonviolent. Would he be capable of a murderous rage if George was threatened? Perhaps. It is through his connection with his intelligent partner that he becomes believable. In the opening scene Steinbeck establishes the dynamics of their relationship, in which George's exasperated bossing of Lennie appears as a form of protectiveness that masks their mutual dependence.

—Anne Loftis, "A Historical Introduction to *Of Mice and Men*." In *The Short Novels of John Steinbeck*, ed. Jackson J. Benson (Durham, NC: Duke University Press, 1990): pp. 41–43.

[William Goldhurst is professor of humanities at the University of Florida. He is the author of *F. Scott Fitzgerald and His Contemporaries* and the editor of *Contours of Experience*. In this excerpt, Goldhurst shows the parallel between *Of Mice and Men* and the biblical story of Cain and Abel.]

Viewed in the light of its mythic and allegorical implications, *Of Mice and Men* is a story about the nature of man's fate in a fallen world, with particular emphasis upon the question: Is man destined to live alone, a solitary wanderer on the face of the earth, or is it the fate of man to care for man, to go his way in companionship with another? This is the same theme that occurs in the Old Testament, as early as chapter 4 of Genesis, immediately following the Creation and Expulsion. In effect, the question Steinbeck poses is the same question Cain poses to the Lord: "Am I my brother's keeper?" From its position in the scriptural version of human history we may assume with the compilers of the early books of the Bible that it is the primary *question concerning man as he is,* after he has lost the innocence and nonbeing of Eden. It is the same question that Steinbeck chose as the theme of his later book *East of Eden* (1952), in which the Cain and Abel story is reenacted in a contemporary setting and where, for emphasis, Steinbeck has his main characters read the biblical story aloud and comment on it, climaxing the discussion with the statement made by Lee: "I think this is the best-known story in the world because it is everybody's story. I think it is the symbol story of the human soul." *Of Mice and Men* is an early Steinbeck variation on this symbolic story of the human soul. The implications of the Cain and Abel drama are everywhere apparent in the fable of George and Lennie and provide its mythic vehicle.

Contrary to Lee's confident assertion, however, most people know the Cain and Abel story only in general outline. The details of the drama need to be filled in, particularly for the purpose of seeing how they apply to Steinbeck's novella. Cain was a farmer and Adam and Eve's firstborn son. His offerings of agricultural produce to the Lord failed to find favor, whereas the livestock offered by Cain's brother, Abel, was well received. Angry, jealous, and rejected, Cain killed Abel when they were working in the field, and when the Lord inquired of Cain, Where is your brother? Cain replied: "I know not: Am I my brother's keeper?" For his crime of homicide the Lord banished Cain from his company and from the company of his parents and set upon him a particular curse, the essence of which was that Cain was to become homeless—a wanderer and an agricultural worker who would never possess or enjoy the fruits of his labor. Cain was afraid that other men would hear of his crime and try to kill him, but the Lord marked him in a certain way so as to preserve him from the wrath of others. Thus Cain left home and went to the land of Nod, which, the story tells us, lies east of Eden.

The drama of Cain finds its most relevant application in *Of Mice and Men* in the relationship between Lennie and George, and in the other characters' reactions to their association. In the first of his six scenes Steinbeck establishes the two ideas that will be developed throughout. The first of these is the affectionate symbiosis of the two protagonists, their brotherly mutual concern and faithful companionship. Steinbeck stresses the beauty, joy, security, and comfort these two derive from the relationship:

> "If them other guys gets in jail they can rot for all anybody
> gives a damn. But not us."
>   Lennie broke in, "But not us! An' why? Because . . .
> because I got you to look after me and you got me to look
> after you, and that's why." He laughed delightedly.

The second idea, which is given equal emphasis, is the fact that this sort of camaraderie is rare, different, almost unique in the world George and Lennie inhabit; other men, in contrast to these two, are solitary souls without friends or companions. Says George in scene 1: "Guys like us, that work on ranches, are the loneliest guys in the world. They got no family. They don't belong no place. They come to a ranch an' work up a stake and then they go into town and blow their stakes, and the first thing you know they're poundin' their tail on some other ranch." The alternative to the George-Lennie companionship is Aloneness, made more dreadful by the addition of an economic futility that Steinbeck augments and reinforces in later sections. The migratory ranch worker, in other words, is the fulfillment of the Lord's curse on Cain: "When thou tillest the ground, it shall not henceforth yield unto thee her strength; a fugitive and vagabond shalt thou be in the earth." Steinbeck's treatment of the theme is entirely free from a sense of contrivance; all the details in *Of Mice and Men* seem natural in the context and organically related to the whole; but note that in addition to presenting Lennie and George as men who till the ground and derive no benefits from their labor, he also manages to have them "on the run" when they are introduced in the first scene—this no doubt to have his main characters correspond as closely as possible to the biblical passage: "a fugitive and a vagabond shalt thou be...."

—William Goldhurst, "*Of Mice and Men:* John Steinbeck's Parable of the Curse of Cain." In *The Short Novels of John Steinbeck*, ed. Jackson J. Benson (Durham, NC: Duke University Press, 1990): pp. 51–53.

Mark Spilka on Steinbeck's Treatment of Curley's Wife

[Mark Spilka is professor of English and comparative literature at Brown University. His works include *The Love Ethic of D. H. Lawrence* and *Hemingway's Quarrel with Androgyny*. In this excerpt, Spilka discusses the differences in the character of Curley's wife in the novel *Of Mice and Men* and in the theater version of the story.]

⟨ . . . ⟩ Steinbeck projects his own hostilities through George and Lennie. He has himself given this woman no other name but "Curley's wife," as if she had no personal identity for him. He has presented her, in the novel, as vain, provocative, vicious (she threatens Crooks with lynching, for instance, when he tries to defy her), and only incidentally lonely. Now in the play—perhaps in response to the criticisms of friends—he reverses her portrait. She is no longer vicious (her lynching threat has been written out of the script), and she is not even provocative: she is just a lonely woman whose attempts at friendliness are misunderstood. Thus she makes her first entrance with a line transferred from a later scene in the novel: "I'm just lookin' for somebody to talk to," she says, in case we might think otherwise. In her final scene, moreover, in a sympathy speech written expressly for the play, she joins Lennie in the lost world of childhood:

CURLEY'S WIFE: My ol' man was a sign-painter when he worked. He used to get drunk an' paint crazy pitchers an' waste paint. One night when I was a little kid, him an' my ol' lady had an awful fight. They was always fightin'. In the middle of the night he come into my room, and he says, "I can't stand this no more. Let's you an' me go away." I guess he was drunk. *(Her voice takes on a curious wondering tenderness.)* I remember in the night—walkin' down the road, and the trees was black. I was pretty sleepy. He picked me up, an' he carried me on his back. He says, "We gonna live together. We gonna live together because you're my own little girl, an' not no stranger. No arguin' and fightin'," he says, "because you're my little daughter." *(Her voice becomes soft.)* He says, "Why you'll bake little cakes for me, and I'll paint pretty pitchers all over the wall." *(Sadly.)* In the morning they caught us . . . an' they put him away. *(Pause.)* I wish we'd a' went.

Here Steinbeck overcompensates, creates a new imbalance to correct an old one. His sentimentality is the obverse side of his hostility. We see this in the novel when it breaks through in another form, as a mystic moment of redemption for Curley's wife. Thus, as she lies dead in the barn, "the meanness and the plannings and the discontent and the ache for attention" disappear from her face; she becomes sweet and young, and her rouged cheeks and reddened lips make her seem alive and sleeping lightly "under a half-covering of hay." At which point sound and movement stop, and, "as sometimes happens," a moment settles and hovers and remains "for much, much more than a moment." Then time wakens and moves sluggishly on. Horses stamp in the barn, their halter chains clink, and outside, men's voices become "louder and clearer."

Restored to natural innocence through death, Curley's wife is connected—for a timeless moment—with the farm dream. Then men's voices and stamping horses indicate the sexual restlessness she provokes in adult life. Only when sexually quiescent—as in death or childhood—can she win this author's heart.

—Mark Spilka, "Of George and Lennie and Curley's Wife: Sweet Violence in Steinbeck's Eden." In *The Short Novels of John Steinbeck,* ed. Jackson J. Benson (Durham, NC: Duke University Press, 1990): pp. 64–66.

JEAN EMERY ON MISOGYNY IN *OF MICE AND MEN*

[Jean Emery has contributed essays and research on various subjects relating to feminist studies. In this excerpt, Emery discusses the feminine role in *Of Mice and Men*.]

Of Mice and Men is not, as most critics would have us believe, a poignant, sentimental drama of an impossible friendship and an unattainable dream. Rather, the story actually demonstrates the achievement of a dream—that of a homogeneous male fraternity not just to repress, but to eliminate women and femininity. *Of Mice and Men* depicts the rescue of men from women, "a melodrama of beset manhood," to use the words of Nina Baym.

Textual evidence suggests that John Steinbeck, as chronicler of America's social inequities, intended *Of Mice and Men* as a critique of our society's most fundamental injustice. George and Lennie represent the duality of masculinity and femininity, their partnership a kind of marriage. Ultimately, George's need and desire to confirm his membership in the powerful and dominant male community drives him to kill his partner as a sacrificial rite of initiation. Bolstered by smaller, less dramatic, but nonetheless significant sacrifices, the text illustrates the insidious presence of this practice in our culture at large. That for more than 50 years literary critics have read the text purely as an exposé of a failed *economic* dream corroborates a blindness to this issue and complicity in preserving the patriarchy.

George and Lennie as a couple display the stereotypical attributes of husband and wife. Lennie's refrain, "I got you to look after me, and you got me to look after you," solemnizes a kind of marriage vow between them. "We got a future," George says in reply. The glue that binds George and Lennie is the dream of a house and a couple of acres where they can "live off the fatta the lan'." George, the masculine creator of this dream, gives it voice and grounds it in the realm of possibility. But it is "feminine" Lennie who nurtures it and keeps it alive with his boundless obsession for hearing George tell it "like you done before."

As in many traditional marriages, this is not a partnership of equals but one of lord and vassal, owner and owned. George as the patriarch makes the decisions, controls the finances, decides where they'll work and live, dictates the conditions of the relationship ("no rabbits" is the threat employed), even regulates when Lennie can and cannot speak. Yet George wants power without the burden of responsibility. "God, you're a lot of trouble," he says more than once to Lennie. "I could get along so easy and so nice if I didn't have you on my tail."

George's droning retelling of the dream is done primarily for Lennie's benefit. George's own dream is really something quite different: "If I was alone I could live so easy. I could go get a job an' work, an' no trouble. No mess at all, and when the end of the month come I could take my fifty bucks and go into town and get whatever I want." The latent message, of course, is that life would be better without the complications of a relationship of a dependent "other."

Relationships in this story center on the issue of power: who will have it and who will not. Obsessed with his ability to control Lennie's behavior (just as Curley is driven to regulate his wife's), George admonishes Lennie for carrying dead mice in his pocket, for directly responding to a question from the Boss, for bringing a pup into the bunkhouse. Such power frightens and, at the same time, thrills George. "Made me seem God damn smart alongside him," George tells Slim. "Why he'd do any damn thing I tol' him. If I tol' him to walk over a cliff, over he'd go." George then recounts the time Lennie nearly drowned demonstrating exactly such obedience.

Peter Lisca suggests that George needs Lennie as a rationalization for his own failure. But George's failure is not just his inability to establish his own autonomy. It is also his struggle to assure himself of his own masculinity and reject the disturbing influence of such feminine traits as gentleness, compassion, submissiveness, and weakness. Lennie's size and strength, a constant reminder of George's own physical puniness, presents a constant threat to George's vulnerable masculinity, clearly displayed in Lennie's effortless emasculation of Curley when Lennie crushes the bully's hand.

Demonstrations of masculinity suffuse the text. The ranch George and Lennie come to work—a stronghold of physical effort, rationality, and orderliness—reeks with maleness. The bunkhouse, utilitarian and void of decoration except for "those Western magazines ranch men love to read and scoff at and secretly believe," exemplifies the heroic male struggle to control nature, other men, and, inevitably, women.

Woman and, correspondingly, feminine traits are intruders and threats to this world, "entrappers" and "domesticators" in Baym's words, woman as temptress thwarting man in his journey of self-discovery and definition.

—Jean Emery, "Manhood Beset: Misogyny in *Of Mice and Men*," *San Jose Studies* 18, no. 1 (Winter 1992): pp. 38–39.

LELAND S. PERSON JR. ON THE DREAM OF A MALE UTOPIA

[Leland S. Person Jr. is a professor of English at Southern Illinois University at Carbondale. His essays have appeared in various scholarly journals, including the *Steinbeck Newsletter*. In this excerpt, Person discusses communalism in *Of Mice and Men*.]

In contrast, the "little house" dream that George and Lennie regularly invoke features democratic cooperation and communalism—an all-male version of the matriarchy that Warren Motley has detected in Ma Joad's role in *The Grapes of Wrath*. The two men collaborate dialogically to rehearse a mutual fantasy that subverts the conventionally entrepreneurial "ranch" ideal predicated on owner-worker and subject-object relationships. In effect, the two men share a single subjectivity in the act of collaboration. "You got it by heart," George tells Lennie. "You can do it yourself." But Lennie prefers to supplement George's rhythmical narrative with interpolations of his own—melting his desire into George's in a verbal analogy to Ishmael's mergence of body and mind with other men's in the big tub of sperm. "Someday," George begins, "we're gonna get the jack together and we're gonna have a little house and a couple of acres an' a cow and some pigs and—." "*An' live off the fatta the lan',*" Lennie shouts. "An' have *rabbits*. Go on, George! Tell about what we're gonna have in the garden and about the rabbits in the cages and about the rain in the winter and the stove."

Let me emphasize that what I am calling the homosexual dream is not genitally sexual. Indeed, it depends upon the sublimation of sexual energy in shared labor and homemaking. "We'd have a little house an' a room to ourself," George says. "An' when we put in a crop, why we'd be there to take the crop up. We'd know what come of our planting." Lennie's sexuality, furthermore, is pointedly sublimated in stroking and petting—fantasmatically invested in tending rabbits, traditional symbols of unrestrained sexuality.

Not only does the homosexual dream dissolve competitive relationships, but it attracts and encourages other men to enter imaginatively into an all-male fantasy. Much like Melville, who discovered in the Ishmael-Queequeg bond a "radical potential for social reorganization, based on principles of equality, affection, and respect for the other" [according to Martin], Steinbeck explores alternative economic and social structures through the interdependent bond between George and Lennie. Not unlike Ishmael's revery in "the Squeeze of the Hand," when George and Lennie share the dream with Candy, "They all sat still, all bemused by the beauty of the thing, each mind was popped into the future when this lovely thing should come about." The stoop-shouldered, one-handed Candy volunteers to invest his $350 stake for the chance to "cook and tend the chickens and hoe the garden some"—his proposal reflecting the diversification of gender roles on which such a male utopia would be founded. "An' it'd be our own, an' nobody could can us," George says. "If we don't like a guy we can say 'Get the hell out,' and by God he's got to do it. An' if a fren' come along, why we'd have an extra bunk, an' we'd say, 'Why don't you spen' the night?' and by God he would." George and Lennie's homo-topic dream even dissolves racial barriers, as the crippled stable buck Crooks offers to "work for nothing—just his keep"—if he can be allowed to join them. "A guy needs somebody—to be near him," Crooks says. "Don't make no difference who the guy is, long's he's with you."

—Leland S. Person Jr., "*Of Mice and Men*: Steinbeck's Speculation in Manhood," *Steinbeck Newsletter*, Winter/Spring 1995. Reprinted in *Readings on Of Mice and Men*, ed. Jill Karson (San Diego, CA: The Greenhaven Press, 1998): pp. 124–126.

Works by John Steinbeck

Cup of Gold: A Life of Sir Henry Morgan, Buccaneer,
with Occasional Reference to History. 1932.

The Pastures of Heaven. 1932.

To a God Unknown. 1933.

Tortilla Flat. 1935.

In Dubious Battle. 1936.

Of Mice and Men. 1937.

The Red Pony. 1937.

Their Blood Is Strong. 1938.

The Long Valley. 1939.

The Grapes of Wrath. 1939.

Sea of Cortez: A Leisurely Journal of Travel and Research
with a Scientific Appendix. Coauthored with Edward F. Ricketts. 1941.

The Forgotten Village. 1941.

Bombs Away: The Story of a Bomber Team. 1942.

The Moon Is Down. 1942.

The Moon Is Down: A Play in Two Parts. 1942.

Cannery Row. 1945.

The Wayward Bus. 1947.

The Pearl. 1947.

A Russian Journal. 1948.

Burning Bright. 1950.

The Log from "The Sea of Cortez." 1951.

East of Eden. 1952.

Sweet Thursday. 1954.

The Short Reign of Pippin IV: A Fabrication. 1957.

Once There Was a War. 1958.

The Winter of Our Discontent. 1961.

Travels with Charley in Search of America. 1962.

America and Americans. 1966.

Journal of a Novel: The "East of Eden" Letters. 1969.

Viva Zapata! (screenplay of the 1952 film). 1974.

Steinbeck: A Life in Letters. 1975.

The Acts of King Arthur and His Noble Knights: From the Winchester Manuscript and Other Sources. 1976.

Working Days: The Journal of "The Grapes of Wrath." 1988.

Works about
John Steinbeck

Adams, James Donald. "Main Street and the Dust Bowl." In *Shape of Books to Come*. New York, 1944: 131–143.

Alexander, Stanley Gerald. "Primitivism and Pastoral Form in John Steinbeck's Early Fiction." *DAI* 26 (1965): 2201A–2202A.

Astro, Richard. *John Steinbeck and Edward F. Ricketts: The Shaping of a Novelist*. Minneapolis: University of Minnesota Press, 1973.

Benson, Jackson J. "'To Tom, Who Lived It': John Steinbeck and the Man from Weedpatch." *Journal of Modern Literature* 5 (1976): 151–194.

Bloom, Harold, ed. *John Steinbeck*. New York: Chelsea House, 1987.

Carlson, Eric W. "Symbolism in the *Grapes of Wrath*." *College English* 19 (1957–58): 172–175.

Castro, Janice. "Labor Draws an Empty Gun." *Time* (March 26, 1990): 56–59.

Copland, Aaron and Vivian Perlis. *Copland 1900 through 1942*. New York: St. Martin's/Marek, 1984.

Ditsky, John, ed. *Critical Essays on the Grapes of Wrath*. Boston: G. K. Hall, 1989.

———. "John Steinbeck—Yesterday, Today and Tomorrow." *Steinbeck Quarterly* 23 (Winter–Spring 1990): 5–15.

Everson, William K. *The Films of Hal Roach*. Greenwich, Conn.: Museum of Modern Art, New York, 1971.

Fensch, Thomas, ed. *Conversation with John Steinbeck*. Jackson: University of Mississippi Press, 1988.

Fiedler, Leslie. "Looking Back after 50 Years." *San Jose Studies* 16 (Winter 1990): 54–64.

Fontenrose, Joseph. *John Steinbeck: An Introduction and Interpretation*. New York: Holt, Rinehart, and Winston, 1963.

French, Warren. *John Steinbeck*. New York: Twayne, 1961 (rev. ed. 1975).

Gray, James. *John Steinbeck*. Minneapolis: University of Minnesota Press, 1971.

Hyman, Stanley Edgar. "Some Notes on John Steinbeck." *Antioch Review* 2 (1942): 185–200.

Kramer, Mimi. "Tender Grapes." *New Yorker* (April 2, 1990): 87–8 9.

Lisca, Peter. *The Wide World of John Steinbeck.* New Brunswick, NJ: Rutgers University Press, 1958. New York: Gordian Press, 1981.

McGroarty, John Steven. *History of Los Angeles County.* Chicago: American Historical Society, 1923.

Mitchell, Ruth Comfort. *Of Human Kindness.* New York: D. Appleton-Century Co., 1940.

Noble, Donald R., ed. *The Steinbeck Question: New Essays in Criticism.* Troy, NY: Whitson, 1993.

Owens, Louis. *John Steinbeck's Re-Vision of America.* Athens: University of Georgia Press, 1985.

Palmieri, Anthony F. R. "*In Dubious Battle:* A Portrait in Pessimism." *Artes Liberales* 3 (1976): 61–71.

Pratt, John Clark. *John Steinbeck: A Critical Essay.* Grand Rapids, MI: William B. Eerdmans, 1970.

Rombold, Tamara. "Biblical Inversion in *The Grapes of Wrath.*" *College Literature* 14 (1987): 146–166.

Shedd, Margaret. "Of Mice and Men." *Theatre Arts Monthly* 21 (October 1937): 775.

Shillinglaw, Susan. "Carol's Library and Papers." *Steinbeck Newsletter* 2 (Fall 1988): 1–2.

Simmonds, Roy S. *Steinbeck's Literary Achievements.* Muncie, IN: John Steinbeck Society of America, 1976.

Slade, Leonard A., Jr. "The Use of Biblical Allusion in *The Grapes of Wrath.*" *CLA Journal* 11 (1968): 241–2 47.

Taylor, Walter Fuller. "*The Grapes of Wrath* Reconsidered." *Mississippi Quarterly* 12 (1959): 136–144.

Thompson, Ralph. "Revision of *Of Mice and Men.*" *New York Times* (February 27, 1937): 15.

Thurber, James. "What Price Conquest?" Revision of *The Moon Is Down.* *New Republic* (March 16, 1942): 370.

Timmerman, John H. *John Steinbeck's Fiction: The Aesthetics of the Road Taken.* Norman: University of Oklahoma Press, 1986.

————. "The Squatter's Circle in *The Grapes of Wrath.*" *Studies in American Fiction* 17 (1989): 203–211.

Whipple, Thomas K. "Steinbeck: Through a Glass Though Brightly." *New Republic* 90 (October 12, 1938): 274–275.

Wilson, Edmund. "John Steinbeck." In *The Boys in the Back Room.* San Francisco: Colt, 1941, 41–53.

Zollman, Sol. "John Steinbeck's Political Outlook in *The Grapes of Wrath.*" *Literature and Ideology* 13 (1972): 9–20.

Index of
Themes and Ideas